DIVIDING OR STRENGTHENING?

FIVE WAYS OF CHRISTIANITY

By Harry E. Winter, O.M.I.

# DEDICATION

To the Winter (paternal) and Van Wagner (maternal) families, who first taught me about Christians living and loving together;

To the Missionaries Oblates of Mary Immaculate, especially Fr. Jim Sullivan, O.M.I. (1926-2001), who provided me many experiences of meeting and learning about other Christians;

And to the American Society of Missiology, whose annual meetings (1975, 1995-98) showed me that convergence is occurring

# Acknowledgements

This book could never have been written without the friendship of the bishops and presbyterates of the Dioceses of Richmond, VA; Wheeling, WV; Raleigh, NC and especially Buffalo, NY. The librarians Fr. Bonaventure Hayes, O.F.M. and Sr. Tiburtia Gorecki, F.S.S.J. at Christ the King Seminary, East Aurora, NY were most helpful.

Two parishioners deserve special thanks: Emily Kukura, word processor extraordinaire, and Dr. Joan Murzynski, researcher on the Internet of sources and quotes.

Ralph Salerno, owner of Keller Bros. & Miller, Inc., was amazingly helpful during the publishing process.

Bill O'Donnell, O.M.I. made many helpful suggestions as he read every page.

My associate from 1998-2002, Tony Rigoli, O.M.I.'s dedication to producing his book, <u>Funny Things that Happened to Me on the Way to Heaven</u>, helped me persevere in producing this book.

Finding a publisher was very difficult until I thought of Father Nelson Baker (1842-1936) and his presence in the "Cloud of Witnesses" (Hb. 12:1).

Published by:   Harry E. Winter, OMI

Distributed by: Harry E. Winter, OMI
                c/o St. Rose of Lima
                500 Parker Avenue
                Buffalo, NY 14216
                (716) 834-6688 Fax (716) 834-6689
                email: SRLOMI@acsmetro.com
                www.buffomi.org/fiveways.htm

Printed by:    Keller Bros. & Miller, Inc., Buffalo, NY

© 2003 Harry E. Winter, OMI
ISBN: 0-9740702-0-3

# TABLE OF CONTENTS

# INTRODUCTION

There are five ways to live the Christian life. But all five have rarely flourished at the same time. Usually, one or two dominated.

During the last half of the twentieth century, in every denomination, all five competed in the average parish, congregation and religious order. Only once or twice has this happened in the two thousand year history of Christianity. And then, instead of mutual support, the competition brought conflict and division. Yet all five can claim a basis in the New Testament.

Catholic Christians (and they exist in every denomination) are baptized as <u>infants</u>, love the sacraments, and are suspicious of emotion. Evangelical/charismatic Christians search for a born again experience, or baptism in the Spirit, as <u>adults</u>. They welcome emotion, long sermons, witnessing, and are uneasy with structures such as sacraments. Reformed (neo-orthodox) Vatican II Christians recognize the necessity of change and renewal, and frequently mediate between those Christians who practically worship change (liberals) and those who view any change as betrayal (fundamentalists).

We are just beginning to realize that a drastic change occurred across all of Christianity about 1960. Methodist missiologist Gerald Anderson noted that "a teaching conference" was held in Strasbourg, France, for the World Student Christian Federation that year. Four great Protestant theologians found that their speeches "did not seem to give the students what they wanted....'There seemed to be too much speaking about the life of the church; what students wanted was a welcome to this world'."[1]

In 1962, after three years of preparation, the meeting which Roman Catholics consider the 21st ecumenical (world-wide) council began in Rome. Known as the Second Vatican Council (hereafter Vatican II), it included very active participation from Protestant and Eastern Orthodox "observers," and quickly revealed renewal currents which surprised many. First, Catholic reformers showed many similarities to Protestant neo-orthodox Christians. Then, liberal Catholicism emerged after a silence of 50 years. Both the reformers at Vatican II and subsequent liberal Catholics wanted a more positive attitude towards the world.[2]

In 1967, the charismatic movement began to converge with Protestant evangelicalism. Many Catholics and mainstream Protestants started to view evangelicals with new respect.

When Episcopalian Bishop James Pike and Presbyterian Stated Clerk Eugene Carson Blake proposed a Church Unity effort on December 4, 1960, they started what first became known as the Consultation on Church Union (COCU), and by 2002, the Churches Uniting in Christ (CUIC). Over the years, the definition and description of a Church "truly

---

[1] Gerald H. Anderson, "Christian Mission in A.D. 2000: A Glance Backward," Missiology 28 (July 2000, #3): 278.
[2] Catholic (upper case) refers to Roman Catholic; catholic (lower case) refers to those in all churches who love the sacraments, resist emotions, etc.

catholic, truly reformed and truly evangelical" was worked out by members of COCU. I rely a great deal on this description for the three models which occupy the middle of our spectrum (with liberals on the left and fundamentalists on the right). Robert McAfee Brown explains COCU very well.[3]

The fundamentalist and liberal models are described from such general sources as the various editions of Winthrop Hudson's Religion in America[4] and John Deedy's The Catholic Church in the Twentieth Century.[5]

Each of the following chapters is devoted to one of the five ways. I have written for the average church member, who wishes to understand why such variety exists. A supplementary booklet is available for those church members who are leaders in their parish or congregation. This booklet provides sources and development. Parish council members, choir members, lectors, ushers--anyone who is concerned about the effectiveness of Christianity in the new millennium and who intends to read and pray more--will profit from the supplementary booklet. I hope that seminarians and clergy of every denomination will find in these works a valuable refresher course in the challenge these five ways present, from the local congregation to the highest levels of

---

[3] Robert McAfee Brown, The Ecumenical Revolution (Garden City, NY: Anchor Image, rev. ed. 1969), pp. 146-52.

[4] Winthrop S. Hudson, Religion in American (NY: Scribner's, 1965); with John Corrigan (NY: Macmillan, 1992), 5th edition.

[5] John Deedy (ed.), The Catholic Church in the Twentieth Century (Collegeville, MN: Michael Glazier/Liturgical Press, 2000).

administration.

As the 20th century ended, we discovered that many of our seminaries revealed a startling and troubling split. While liberal Christians are probably a small percentage in most denominations, a recent Association of Theological Schools Study stated that in seminaries today, "most teachers are operating out of an anti-foundational, liberal approach." This creates a major problem since most seminarians want core knowledge and solid grounding in their respective denominations, making them much more conservative than their teachers.[6]

Most Christians will readily identify with one way. I call this their "dominant" way. But they will usually have some sympathy for a second way, and some hostility for one of the others, respectively "sympathetic" and "repugnant." Catholics, for example, tend to be uneasy with the need the evangelicals and charismatics have to express their feelings. Fundamentalists reject the flexibility of liberals; liberals reject the stability of fundamentalists. Reformed feel some sympathy with the ability of liberals to adapt. The spectrum diagram at the end of this section may help. The evaluation instrument there is a tool for various groups to identify their way.

Two areas of Christian life are stressed: public worship and mission. In public worship, conflicts over the five ways first arise. Yet if a community can make way for at least three of the five ways, its

---

[6] Susan Willhauck, "ATS Study," The Bulletin, Washington Theological Consortium, Sept. 2000, p. 3.

Christianity will be greatly strengthened.

"The pilgrim Church is missionary by her very nature" is a statement from Vatican II with which most Christians would agree.[7] We have a message and a person to share. Many denominations use some form of the word "evangelism" to express that activity within their own culture. Across cultures, we tend to use the term "mission," to indicate the need to leave one's own culture. One goal of this book is to help all Christians appreciate the different approaches to sharing the message and person of Jesus. Is it possible that the five ways are complimentary, rather than conflictual?

The English born bishop of the Church of South India, Lesslie Newbigin (1909-98) wrote sadly:

> It is a terrifying testimony to the power of sin that even the Gospel can become an instrument of aggression and domination. . . . I vividly remember that when the Indian tanks rolled into what is now called Bangladesh there was an enthusiastic movement in the Church of South India in favor of sending missionaries to that country. . . . To be frank, I am afraid of the strong stench of imperialism, which too often infects the call for world evangelization. Again and again we have to remember the words "He showed them his hands and his side." The authentic bearer of the Gospel is the suffering servant, not the masterful ruler and organizer.[8]

Is it not true that a healthy, vibrant Christianity needs all five ways fully cooperating, if we are to really witness to the Lord? The events of

---

[7] Walter M. Abbott S.J. (gen. Ed.), "Decree on Missionary Activity," #2, Documents of Vatican II (NY: Crossroad, 1989), p. 585.

[8] Lesslie Newbigin, "Cross-currents in Ecumenical and Evangelical Understanding of Mission," (October, 1982), printed in "The Best of Bishop Lesslie Newbigin (New Haven, CT: Overseas Ministries Study Center, 1998), p. 9.

September 11, 2001 demonstrated that the talents of all Christians are needed if we are to minister effectively way to our world.

Members of the Eastern Christian Churches will find that their heritage and contribution are valued in this book. The Christian Church has two lungs, the Eastern and Western, and for Christianity to be healthy, all of us need both lungs.

I write as a Catholic blessed with experiences and friends in many places in Christianity: Eastern, Reformed, Evangelical, Black, Hispanic and Asian. I hope this work will help us respect our rich pluralism as we converge, using the prayer of Jesus "That all may be one, that the world may believe" (Jn. 17:21).

So often Christians ignore the ideas and developments in the other expressions of Christianity. President Ronald Reagan's induction speech into the French Academy, in which he eulogized his predecessor, Cardinal Hans Urs von Balthasar, is a sad example of this tendency. I have included it as appendix one.

On June 2, 2000, Kevin M. Doyle Esq., a Catholic lawyer from New York City who heads the State of NY Public Defender Association, gave the keynote address at the annual dinner of the St. Thomas More Guild, Inc., at the Buffalo, NY Convention Center. I borrow his concluding remark: "I hope you will agree with some of the insights here. But if you agree with all of them, go for counseling immediately."

## Spectrum of Parishes and Congregations

Typical Catholic, Eastern Orthodox, High Episcopal and some Lutheran

| Liberal | Reformed | Catholic | Charismatic | Fundamentalist |
|---------|----------|----------|-------------|----------------|
| 10% | 20% | 30% | 30% | 10% |

Typical Main-stream Protestant (excepting United Church of Christ)

| Liberal | Reformed | Catholic | Evangelical | Fundamentalist |
|---------|----------|----------|-------------|----------------|
| 20% | 25% | 20% | 25% | 10% |

Typical Southern Baptist, Assembly of God, Holiness, and Pentecostal
(Some Missouri Lutheran)

| Liberal | Reformed | Catholic | Evangelical | Fundamentalist |
|---------|----------|----------|-------------|----------------|
| 5% | 15% | 10% | 35% | 35% |

## An Instrument for Evaluation

Check the one you feel most comfortable with:   (dominant)

Catholic (I Cor. 12:12-28)                 _____

Charismatic/Evangelical  (I Pt. 2:9-10: Rev. 5:8-14    _____

Reformed (Neo-Orthodox) Vatican II (Hb 11-13)     _____

Fundamentalist/Integralist (Rev. 21:10-27)        _____

Liberal (I Pet 2:9-10)                    _____

Check the one you feel most uncomfortable with (repugnant)

Catholic                _____

Charismatic/Evangelical      _____

Reformed (Neo-Orthodox) Vatican II   _____

Fundamentalist/Integralist         _____

Liberal/Modernist             _____

Check the one you feel some sympathy for (sympathetic)

Catholic                _____

Charismatic/Evangelical      _____

Reformed (Neo-Orthodox) Vatican II   _____

Fundamentalist/Integralist         _____

Liberal/Modernist             _____

# CHAPTER ONE: CATHOLIC CHRISTIANITY

## Overview

"I believe in the holy catholic Church" (Apostles Creed).  Christians who follow this way are found in great numbers in the Roman Catholic Church, the Eastern Christian Churches, and in those Episcopalian parishes which are termed "high."  (Outside of the USA, the Episcopal Church is more commonly called the Anglican Church).  Large numbers of the Evangelical Lutheran Church (but not the Missouri Synod) are also catholic.

However, there are also significant numbers of catholics within Methodism, the Presbyterian and Reformed Churches, and even within the Southern Baptist Church.  The expression of James Hastings Nichols that there is an evangelical undertow within Catholicism (see ch. 2) also works the other way:  there is a catholic undertow within evangelicalism.

Predominate characteristics of catholics are a strong suspicion of emotions and feelings; baptism as infants; a love of structure, with an emphasis on the sacraments.  If the Lord's Supper is not already the ordinary Sunday worship service, catholic Christians will go searching for it.  Perhaps the best analysis of the first characteristic, the fear of emotions, was done by the English Catholic Scripture scholar and retreat master, Monsignor Ronald Knox (1888-1957), in his classic and oft-reprinted Enthusiasm.

Religion became identified in the popular mind with a
series of moods, in which the worshipper, disposed thereto,
by all the arts of the revivalist, relished the flavors of
spiritual peace. You needed neither a theology nor a liturgy;
you did not take the strain of intellectual inquiry, nor
associate yourself wholeheartedly with any historic tradition
of worship. You floated, safely enough, on a little raft of your
own faith, eagerly throwing out the lifeline to such drowning
neighbors as were ready to catch it; meanwhile the ship was
foundering.[1]

## Scripture Image and Implications

As Knox revealed in his picture of the Church as the ship,

catholics are very concerned about the universal Church. They

instinctively view it as the Body of Christ, resorting to Paul's rich imagery

in I Cor. 12:4-27. COCU, by 1980, had developed this.[2] And when Pope

Pius XII published his encyclical (the highest kind of papal document

short of an infallible statement) Mystici Corporis (The Mystical Body) in

the dark days of World War II (1943), he startled many Christians by the

rich Biblical theology of the Church, which undergirded the encyclical.

When Vatican II developed its foundation document Constitution on the

Church, it devoted two lengthy sections (7-8) to the Church as Christ's

Body.

The growth of the human body is slow and predictable, which suits

catholic Christians very much. And they sense that some parts of the

body are more important than others. The clergy and nuns are somehow

---

[1] Ronald A. Knox, Enthusiasm, A Chapter in the History of Religion (Notre Dame, IN: University of Notre Dame Press, 1994), p. 589.
[2] COCU, In Quest of a Church Unity , (Princeton, NJ: COCU, 1980), pp. 13-15.

more important, to the catholic mind, than the laity. This means that evangelization is often left to the clergy. Even the lay-led groups in Catholicism, such as the Legion of Mary, the St. Vincent de Paul Society and the Catholic Worker Movement, tend to be very well organized and very structured, sometimes to the detriment of lay initiative.

The great lay leaders of the Greek Orthodox Church in the 1950's, Leon Zander and Nikos Nissiotis, typify how painfully lay leadership learns to work with the clergy. It is not an easy experience, but one that catholics elaborate on, with some anti-clericalism (usually expressed with a smile), such as Frank Sheed (1897-1981) in his sometimes autobiography The Church and I.[3]

The best short criticism of this reluctance by catholics to evangelize is Cardinal Avery Dulles' widely circulated 1991 McGinley lecture "Why Catholics Don't Evangelize and Why They Must."[4]

Catholics emphasize that the institutional elements of Christianity were present from the beginning. Presbyterian Scripture scholar George Buttrick found "unmistakable allusions to the Eucharist" in John 6.[5] Swiss Reformed theologian Oscar Cullmann demonstrated that the establishment of Peter as the leader of the twelve in Matthew 16:18 is

[3] Frank Sheed, The Church and I, (Garden City, NJ: Doubleday, 1974), pp. 13-15.
[4] Avery Dulles, S.J., "Why Catholics Don't Evangelize and Why They Must," America, Feb. 1, 1992, 52-59, 69-72, reprinted by the National Office of the Propagation of the Faith, 366 Fifth Ave., New York, NY 10001, 1-800-431-222; 212-563-8700, www.propfaith.org and e-mail profaith@aol.com. The videos and publications by this organization are remarkable; Father Eugene LaVerdiere, S.S.S. "Gospel series" explaining "The Mission of the Church: . . .According to Matthew," ". . .According to Mark," and ". . .According to Luke" are excellent for a sense of mission.
[5] George A. Buttrick, Interpreter's Bible (NY: Abingdon, 1952), 8:567 (also 562-63).

embedded in the deepest Hebrew layer of Matthew, and not a later Greek interpretation as liberals once pushed.[6] And of course the Acts of the Apostles and the three pastoral epistles (I and II Timothy and Titus) show a community developing structured leadership from widows to bishops, presbyters and deacons.

Catholics are unanimous in rejecting the Church as a voluntary organization. The Church is not a religious Elks, Rotary or neighborhood help group. As the Dominican historian Yves Congar has demonstrated, somehow "the mystery of the Church was already in part established and made known . . . . with God's promises to Abraham."[7] So the Church exerts its influence long before we join it; our actions, in a very real sense, do not affect it. Ronald Rolheiser is certain about this sad tendency: "We want God, but we don't want church." And he is certain that community is a non-negotiable part of Christianity, because Christ, God, took flesh, became incarnate--hence the term incarnation. Catholics sense that "We are the Body of Christ. This is not a exaggeration, nor a metaphor."[8]

Because of this Scriptural emphasis on the community first (before the individual), Catholics want reverence during worship. If the community makes rules and regulations, then these are presumed to be

---

[6] Oscar Cullmann, Peter, Apostle and Martyr, (Philadelphia: PA: 1962), rev. ed. For the liberals, see Nichols below, chap. 5.
[7] Yves Congar O.P., Mystery of the Church (Baltimore, MD: Helicon, 1965), 2nd, rev. ed., pp. 15-16.
[8] Ronald Rolheiser, O.M.I., The Holy Longing, (NY: Doubleday, 1999), pp. 68-78.

valuable and purposeful. A Presbyterian liturgist insisted in 1944: "The Order should not be tampered with. The minister should not introduce experiments into the service. He should let the Sacrament speak. . . . Too often regarding this there is a carelessness and irreverence, which is frequently noticed by the people and especially by the young."[9]

Kerr put into words what many catholics feel: the sacraments have a certain superiority over preaching. "Before the Gospels were written . . . the early Christians were celebrating the sacraments . . . . There is, however, less occasion for failure in the celebration of the sacraments," since they "are objective and do not depend upon the preacher's 'feelings' or upon his intellectual apprehension."[10] Sermons in catholic parishes may last only 10 minutes, and the congregation does not feel cheated.

COCU noted that catholics are very conscious of sharing "in the communion of saints which extends over the whole world and throughout all ages."[11] This means that not only are people venerated as vehicles of Jesus' love, but matter too: sacraments, sacramentals, such as holy water, blessed oil, icons, statues, rosaries, etc.

Note that the word "communion," with its poor English translation of "fellowship," has a significant and important Biblical and Patristic heritage. Catholics and Methodists affirmed in 1986:

---

[9] Hugh Thomson Kerr, Sr., Christian Sacraments, (Philadelphia, PA: Westminster, 1944), pp. 96-97, 106.
[10] Ibid., pp. 27-29, 146.
[11] COCU, In Quest, p. 13.

Koinonia is so rich a term that it is better to keep its original Greek form than bring together several English words to convey its meaning. For believers it involves both communion and community. It includes participation in God through Christ in the Spirit by which believers become adopted children of the same Father and members of the one Body of Christ sharing in the same Spirit. And it includes deep fellowship among participants, a fellowship which is both visible and invisible, finding expression in faith and order, in prayer and sacrament, in mission and service.[12]

Father Francis A. Sullivan prefers the word participation, "because it is the English word that comes closest to the original meaning of the Greek word koinonia." In an easily accessible and masterful explanation of Pope John Paul II's use of the word, Sullivan recalls how St. Paul uses the concept in a worship setting: "The cup of blessing that we bless, is it not a participation (koinonia) in the blood of Christ? The bread that we break, is it not a participation (koinonia) in the body of Christ?" (I Cor. 10:16)[13]

Brother Jeff Gros has collected the basic texts concerning koinonia in his Introduction to Ecumenism.[14] An Italian priest who is very impressed by the Focolare Movement (see below, p. 19) has recently published a work on koinonia which examines the concept from the viewpoint of religious communities, some of them very untraditional.[15]

---

[12] J.M.R. Tillard O.P., "Commentary on 'Towards a Statement on the Church'," One in Christ, 22 (1986, #3): 262, citing #4; see also #1 (p. 260).
[13] Francis A. Sullivan, S.J., "The Magisterium in the New Millennium," America, Aug. 27, 2001, pp. 13-14.
[14] Jeffrey Gros, F.S.C., Eamon McManus and Ann Riggs, Introduction to Ecumenism, (N.Y.: Paulist, 1998), pp 57-73 and passim.
[15] Fabio Ciardi, O.M.I., Koinonia: Spiritual and Theological Growth of the Religious Community (Hyde Park, NY: New City Press, 2001).

## Historical Overview

COCU's "throughout all ages" finds catholics esteeming certain historical times more than others. Evangelicals stress the periodic but unpredictable revivals which explode within Christianity, beginning with the holy men and women in the third century desert areas. But catholics note that each of these enthusiastic waves needed rules, constitutions, and structure, usually leaving behind religious orders of men and women. And each revival eventually affected worship.

The Trappist author Thomas Merton gives a short but memorable view of the excesses and reforms in his history of the Trappist order Waters of Siloe.[16] For Catholics, James J. Walsh expressed the golden age as the Middle Ages, when Church and State worked closely together.[17] For Greek Orthodox, those moments when Patriarch (of Constantinople) and Emperor were cooperating harmoniously, are precious.[18] Catholics tend to believe that a transformation of society by Christian principles is possible. COCU elaborated when it described the catholic quality: "The Church seeks to inform the whole realm of culture and society with the spirit of Christ. . . .inspiring new expressions in philosophy, literature, music and the arts, as well as social reform."[19]

---

[16] Thomas Merton, Waters of Siloe, (NY: Harcourt, 1949, pp. 3-31).

[17] James J. Walsh, The Thirteenth Greatest of Centuries, (NY: Fordham U. Press, 1907, 1952). Deedy, The Catholic Church in the Twentieth Century shows the importance of Walsh: pp. ix-x.

[18] See John Meyendorff, The Orthodox Church (Crestwood, NY: St. Vladimir's Press, 1962), pp. 19-25, 59-60.

[19] COCU, In Quest, p. 15.

Note that evangelism and mission will have a less individualistic and more societal focus, compared to the evangelicals and charismatics of chapter 2 below.

The catholic undertow within Christianity is especially noteworthy since the Oxford Movement arose in Anglicanism and brought John Henry Newman into Catholicism. Similar movements occurred at the same time within German Lutheranism and even American Presbyterian-Reformed (the remarkable Mercersburg Theology). James Hastings Nichols wrote about the two Mercersburg leaders, John Williamson Nevin (1803-86) and Philip Schaff (1819-93):

> They were the chief spokesman in America for that traditionalist, "churchly", sacramental movement which swept across much of Christendom in the second generation of the nineteenth century. What Moehler meant to Roman Catholicism, Khomiakov to Russian Orthodoxy, Lohe and Kliefoth to Lutheranism, or Newman, Pusey, and Wilberforce to the Church of England--that was akin to what Nevin and Schaff meant to the dominant Reformed and Puritan tradition in America. There were Episcopalians and Lutherans in the United States who belonged to this same romantic current, but none compare with Nevin and Schaff in intellectual power or in scholarship.[20]

## Current Situation

Recently, a number of very high profile evangelicals have joined Eastern Orthodox Churches, such as former workers in Campus

---

[20] James Hastings Nichols, Romanticism in American Theology, (Chicago, IL: U. of Chicago Press, 1961), p. 3. See also his The Mercersburg Theology, (New York: Oxford U. Press, 1966), Library of Protestant Thought 8.

Crusade for Christ, and Frankie Shaeffer of the L'Abri Fellowship.[21]
Southern Baptist John Claypool became a priest in the Episcopal
Church.[22]  Scott Hahn, a Presbyterian minister, found a home in the
Catholic Church.[23]

Within those denominations where catholics are a strong plurality,
one finds a spectrum, ranging from those on the left, sympathetic to
liberal issues, to those on the right, sympathetic to fundamentalist
issues.  Within the Presbyterian-Reformed tradition, for example, one
finds two groups insisting on the weekly Lord's Supper, Scotland's Iona
Community and France's Taizē Community.  (The hymns of both groups
are having an enormous impact on all Churches.)  The L'Abri Fellowship
is much more fundamentalistic, and will be examined in chapter 4.  All
three places attract many, many Americans.

The Swiss Reformed Church produced two theologians fascinated
by the liturgy of the Eastern Church (which of course insists on the
Lord's Supper every Sunday).  Richard Paquier and Jean Jacques von
Allmen form practically a school of their own.  I shall never forget
listening to von Allmen on February 24, 1969, when he lectured to a
packed hall at Princeton Theological Seminary, NJ.  Somewhat perplexed
at von Allmen's orientation towards sacraments and liturgy, one

---

[21] Robert Webber of Wheaton College describes this especially from the attraction of the Vatican II Sunday Lectionary: "Ecumenical Influences on Evangelical Worship," Ecumenical Trends 19 (May 1990, #5) 73-76. See also Vigen Guroian, "Dancing alone--out of step with Orthodoxy," Christian Century, June 7-14, 1995, pp. 608-10, for Shaeffer.

[22] John Claypool, Who's Who in Religion 1992-93, 4th edition, p. 93.

[23] Scott and Kimberly Hahn, Rome Sweet Home (San Francisco, CA: Ignatius Press, 1993).

Presbyterian seminarian bluntly asked him why he remained in the Swiss Reformed Church. Von Allmen smiled and answered, "Because I feel at home, and no one has asked me to leave."

Because of its size, the Catholic Church has the largest number of groups within the spectrum. On the far right are those who went into schism with the late Archbishop Marcel Lefebvre, who will be examined in chapter 4. Close to them, and still hesitatingly in the catholic camp, are those who make the Tridentine Latin Mass their touchstone, the Priestly Fraternity of St. Peter. One of their sympathizers, Rev. Albert M. Liberatore wrote a very irenic article in America, attempting to bring mainstream Catholics and the Fraternity closer together.[24] While exact figures are hard to come by, it does seem that sympathizers of the Tridentine Mass are growing in number. In 1990, six USA dioceses allowed the Mass; in 1994, 70 dioceses; in 2000, 131.[25]

Other Catholics ask why not use the Vatican II Mass in Latin, as is done at the Cathedral of St. Matthew, Washington, DC, every Sunday?[26] If reverence is desired, and attention to the tradition behind the Tridentine Mass, this would seem to suffice.

The Wanderer weekly newspaper and its sister organization "Catholics United for the Faith" (CUF) would be close to the right edge,

---

[24] Albert M. Liberatore, "Beyond Nightmares and Dreams: Trent and Vatican II," America, April 16, 1994, pp. 16-17.
[25] AP account of growth in Erie, PA diocese, Buffalo News 1-27-00, p. A-11; NC Register, 9-24-00, p.2.
[26] Rev. Msgr. W. Ronald Jameson to Harry Winter, July 10, 2002.

along with Mother Angelica and her EWTN television and radio complex. The Legionnaires of Christ, who took over the moderate national weekly newspaper The Catholic Register in 1995, voice a strongly "restorationist" agenda, as some term it.[27]

Richard John Neuhaus and his journal First Things; the New Oxford Review; the Fellowship of Catholic Scholars Quarterly, and Crisis Magazine of Ralph McInerny and Michael Novak all articulate the catholic position. Communio and Traces (the magazine of Msgr. Luigi Giussani's international lay movement Communion and Liberation (CL)) bring us to the left edge, where we find groups such as the Catholic Worker Movement,[28] and the Community of St. Egidio occupying places similar to Iona and Taizē: the combination of the insistence on a strong sacramental life, with concern and witness to the world for the poor. Mother Teresa's priests and nuns belong here, too.

The Community of St. Egidio has received much favorable press lately. From a beautiful one page editorial in America,[29] to a touching article in NC Register,[30] this lay founded group which stresses both sacraments and international peace efforts demonstrates the vitality of the catholic tendency.

Some would place the Community of St. Egidio, and another

---

[27] For example, Thomas Rausch, S.J., "Divisions, Dialogue and the Catholicity of the Church," America, Jan. 31, 1998.

[28] See George M. Anderson, S.J., "Dorothy Day Centenary, " America, Nov. 29, 1997, pp. 8-10.

[29] "Of Many Things," America, Feb. 19, 2001, p. 2.

[30] "The Magnificat of Terrorists," NC Register, Feb. 11-17, 2001, pp. 15-16.

Italian founded group, Focolare, in the evangelical section. Both are marked by exuberance and feeling. Yet both also are strongly sacramental, insisting on weekly, even daily Mass. Chiara Lubich, Focolare's founder in the bomb shelters of Trent, Italy, during the early 1940's, had always insisted on institutional membership with Catholicism, even as she builds bridges with Eastern Orthodoxy, and Islam.

## Further Characteristics

The priest sociologist Andrew Greeley has popularized the expressions "The Catholic Imagination," and "The Apologetics of Beauty."[31] A material world flawed yet redeemable gives writers and other artists great scope for their talents. From C.S.Lewis (1899-1963) and J.R.R. Tolkien, (1892-1973) to Annie Dillard, the sacramentalism of catholicity has attracted those especially alert to the beauty of this visible world.[32]

Lewis' Mere Christianity probably remains the single most influential explanation of Christianity after the Bible.[33] Dilliard's Pilgrim at Tinker Creek showed her early promise, and interest in religious questions arising from nature. Dillard surprised many in Toronto,

---

[31] See Rose Labrie, The Catholic Imagination in American Literature (U. of Missouri Press, 1998); Andrew M. Greeley, "The Apologetics of Beauty," America, Sept. 16, 2000, pp. 8-14.
[32] See Joseph Pearce, Literary Converts (San Francisco, CA: Ignatius Press, 1999) for a broad description of the English writers. For C.S. Lewis, see Lionel Adey, C.S. Lewis (Grand Rapids, MI: Wm. Eerdmans), 1998.
[33] C.S. Lewis, Mere Christianity (NY: Macmillan, 1960), original 1943.

Canada, when she was confronted by some of the feminists among her followers. They asked her why, of all Churches, she joined the Catholic. She simply stated, "because they accepted me."[34] Or as James Joyce put it, "Catholicism means here comes everybody."[35]

Catholics glory in a certain messiness of the Church. They resist the tendency of evangelicals and charismatics to perfectionism. (Of course this can be carried too far, as it was in the Catholic Church on the eve of the 16th century Reformation).

The harmony of the world is stressed. Continuity, not change attracts them. A robust debate between Cardinal Dulles (stressing continuity) and the late Richard McCormick, S.J. (stressing discontinuity) occurred at the annual meeting of the Catholic Theological Society of America in 1999.[36] The ancient expression of Vincent of Lerins (c100), that we must believe "that which is everywhere, always and by all taught" is characteristic of catholics, no matter what church.[37] For this reason, catholics tend to construct catechisms, summaries of doctrine which are to be held by everyone. The decrees of the first seven ecumenical (world-wide) councils, the Heidelberg Catechism (Reformed Protestants), the Baltimore Catechism and the Catechism of Vatican II

---

[34] Related by Rolheiser, during a retreat in San Antonio, TX, Jan., 1998.

[35] Cited by Cardinal Avery Dulles, S.J., "Catholicism and American Culture," America, Jan. 27, 1990, p. 58 (from Finnegan's Wake).

[36] See David S. Toolan, S.J.'s account, "A Church Bursting with Energy," America, July 17, 1999, pp. 7-8, and previously, "Letters to Editor," May 29, July 3, July 31.

[37] Yves Congar O.P. examines this expression in Diversity and Communion (Mystic, CT: Twenty-third Publications, 1985), pp. 123-25. See also Liturgy of the Hours (NY: Catholic Book Publishing Co., 1975) 4:363, (Office of Readings, Friday, 27 Week of Ordinary Times).

(Catholic), the soon-to-be published catechism for Presbyterians in the USA--all reflect the catholic need to have a world-wide system of beliefs.

The debate between catholics and evangelicals over the need for structure has been going on for centuries. J.H. Nichols summed up one truth when he wrote that structures, especially "Eucharistic practice," do not necessarily prevent decay, but they do facilitate renewal.[38] And Kerr warned evangelicals that what seemed to them to be "extempore prayer," without patterns, very quickly developed into patterns that require a great deal of preparation (sometimes to appear without preparation).[39]

Two things are clear: the catholic development of structure in worship has been growing across all churches. The COCU 1968 Order of Worship proposed prayers for the dead, worshipping "with the whole company of saints in heaven and on earth," suggests kneeling during the institution account, speaks of the congregation offering themselves and presenting holy gifts, and as a clincher suggests reserving the "blessed" bread and wine for communion of the sick.[40]

Presbyterians and others who attend Princeton (NJ) Seminary began celebrating the Easter Vigil in the 1970's, from dusk to dawn.[41] And Harold M. Daniels, editor of the Book of Common Worship, can now

---

[38] J.H. Nichols, Corporate Worship in the Reformed Tradition, (Philadelphia, PA: Westminster Press, 1969), p. 141.

[39] H.T. Kerr, "Study of the Book of Common Worship," Journal of the Presbyterian Historical Society, 29 (1951): 211, also 30, 32.

[40] An Order of Worship, (Cincinnati: Forward Movement Publications, 1968).

[41] Arlo Duba, "Development of Paschal Vigil at Princeton Theological Seminary," Liturgy 19 (Jan. 1974): 3-8.

state that "a significant contribution of the new <u>Book of Common</u>

<u>Worship</u> (1993) is the recovery of the centrality of the paschal mystery,

expressed in the Three Great Days (triduum)."[42]

The Presbyterian Church (USA) has found that the frequency of the

Lord's Supper, from 1990-97, has increased from 42 to 55% for

congregations celebrating the Lord's Supper "monthly or more often." [43]

Presbyterian elder Colonel Edwin E. Aldrin, Jr. showed a catholic

instinct when he celebrated Communion on the moon.   This is how he

described it, after landing on the moon and before the famous moonwalk.

> I had one ceremony I'd planned.  My pastor at Webster
> Presbyterian Church in Houston had given me a tiny
> communion kit, complete with miniature silver chalice and a
> wine vial about the size of my little fingertip.  I asked ". . .
> every person listening in, whoever and wherever they may
> be, to pause for a moment and contemplate the events of the
> past few hours, and to give thanks in his or her own way."
>     The clear plastic shelf in front of our DSKY (sic) became
> the altar.  I read silently from the communion service, "I am
> the vine and you are the branches" . . . as I poured the wine
> into the chalice.  The wine looked like syrup as it swirled
> around the sides of the cup in the light gravity before it
> finally settled at the bottom.
>     Eagle's metal body creaked faintly.  I ate the tiny host
> and swallowed the wine.  I gave thanks for the intelligence
> and spirit that had brought two young pilots to the Sea of
> Tranquility.[44]

Seth Borenstein, writing in 1998 for the Knight Ridder News

---

[42] Harold M. Daniels, "Book of Common Worship (1993):  What's New," <u>Reformed Liturgy & Music</u> 27 (1993, 4): 22.

[43] Jack Marcum to Harry Winter, July 14, 2000, PC (USA) Research services reported in Harry E. Winter, O.M.I., "Presbyterians Pioneer the Vatican II Sunday Lectionary," <u>Journal of Ecumenical Studies</u> 38 (Spring-Summer, 2001, #2-3): 148..

[44] Buzz Aldrin and Malcolm McConnell, "Men from Earth," Book Section of <u>Reader's Digest,</u> July, 1989, p. 205.  For Werner Von Braun and the Lord's Prayer, see p. 34.  <u>Presbyterian Life</u>, See. 1969, p. 6, and <u>Life Magazine</u>, Aug 22, 1969, p. 27 noted the Communion service.  An attempt to contact Colonel Aldrin at Random House, publisher of his 1973 <u>Return to Earth</u> (see pp. 232-33) went unanswered.

Agency about the effect of "faith" on astronauts, stated "The first liquid poured and food eaten on the moon occurred when Buzz Aldrin took Communion."[45]

## Spirituality

The author who best summarizes catholic spirituality is the Trappist priest M. Eugene Boylan, in <u>This Tremendous Lover</u>, first published in 1947.[46] The hardcover edition contained a valuable appendix on the classics in Christian spirituality "Spiritual Reading" (pp. 338-45). The paperback version, which unfortunately does not contain the appendix, has been reprinted over 31 times, and is currently available through Thomas More Publishers.[47]

It should be noted that Boylan was no hermit. As a young student from Ireland in Nazi Germany, studying nuclear physics, he faced squarely the challenges of that time, and decided that confronting himself and his brethren in Trappist monasteries both in Ireland and Australia was where God wanted him. His books breath a great knowledge of himself, God and the world.

More recently, the German Catholic priest, F.X. Durrwell appealed to catholics with <u>In the Redeeming Christ</u>, using even more tools of the

---

[45] Seth Borenstein, Knight Ridder News Agency, Space Center, Houston, Nov. 7, 1998, Buffalo (NY) News.
   [46] M. Eugene Boylan, O.C.S.O., <u>This Tremendous Lover</u>, (Westminister, MD: Newman Press, 1947).
   [47] Boylan, <u>This Tremendous Lover</u>, (Westminster, MD: Christian Classics, 1964, reprinted most recently in 1987).

modern Scripture movement than Boylan did.[48]

Believers are not surprised when changes in worship provoke very emotional reactions. The Russian Orthodox Church had a schismatic response when the sign of the cross was changed from left to right.[49] And Catholics are very familiar with the fearful response of some to the sweeping changes in the Mass made by Vatican II.

We shall examine the controversy over Vatican II more thoroughly in chapters 3-5. Here, we must call attention to the change in two very early proponents of Vatican II: Joseph Ratzinger, and Andrew Greeley.

Ratzinger was a young "peritus" (theologian officially appointed to participate and advise) at the council. By 1982, he had moderated his earlier attitude. In 1962, he quoted for his German bishops a very enthusiastic text from Eusebius of Caesarea, who had participated in the First Ecumenical Council, Nicaea I (325). But in 1982, he called this text "triumphalistic," and unthinkable. He had now discovered texts from Gregory of Nazianzus, reflecting on his experience at the Second Ecumenical Council, Constantinople I (381), observing: "Every assembly of bishops is to be avoided, for I have never experienced a happy ending to any council; not even the abolition of abuses. . . , but only ambition or wrangling." Ratzinger joined Basil the Great's comment: "'shocking disorder and confusion' of the conciliar disputes, of the 'incessant

---

[48] F.X. Durrwell, C.SS.R., In the Redeeming Christ, (N.Y.: Sheed and Ward, 1963).
[49] Meyendorff, The Orthodox Church, pp. 109-10; Roberson, The Eastern Churches, 121-23.

chatter' that filled the whole Church."[50]

Even more surprising has been the evolution of Father Greeley. His 2001 article "A Cloak of Many Colors: The End of Beige Catholicism" attracted much comment. He did not want to restore catholic worship practice from before Vatican II, but did strongly suggest that "the church, in its haste to adjust to the postconciliar world, jettisoned much of what was distinctive and precious in the Catholic sacramental heritage." He singled out four areas for reinstitution: Plain song, statues, the rosary and meatless Fridays.[51]

Catholics can become fussy and even bewildered by too much development; pruning back (Jo 15:1-8 for the vine and branches) is regularly needed. My Episcopalian friends tease their high Church (or Anglo-Catholic) liturgists, who are so hung up on accessories like incense, that instead of using incense at Mass, they use Mass at incense. Many Catholics feel that if one genuflection shows reverence, ten show more reverence. This leads to the conclusion that the only difference between a liturgist and a terrorist is that you can at least negotiate with the terrorist.[52]

On a deeper level, the neo-orthodox theologian Richard Kroner, who resembled Paul Tillich in many ways (escaping from Nazi Germany,

---

[50] Joseph Ratzinger, Principles of Catholic Theology (San Francisco, CA: Ignatius Press, 1987, German original, 1982), pp. 367-69.

[51] Andrew M. Greeley, "A Cloak of Many Colors," Commonweal, Nov. 9, 2001, p. 10, condensed in Catholic Digest, June, 2002, pp. 19-27, and commented on by David E. Nantals, S.J., "Retro-Catholicism," America, May 20, 2002, pp. 16-17.

[52] No one has claimed the authorship of this saying.

etc.), observed that the papacy set out to baptize the great gifts of Renaissance humanism. Instead, he believes the papacy of that time became corrupted by the good life of the Renaissance.[53] Both reformed and evangelicals criticize catholics for failing to sometimes see and evade the dangers of fallen creation, for elevating the material to near idolatry.

Even Ronald Knox, for all his fear of enthusiasm, ends his book with these observations:

> More than all the other Christianities, the Catholic Church is institutional. . . .But there is danger in her position none the less; where wealth abounds, it is easy to mistake shadow for substance; the fires of spirituality may burn low, and we go on unconscious, dazzled by the glare of tinsel suns. How nearly we thought we could do without St. Francis, without St. Ignatius. Men will not live without vision; that moral we do well to carry away with us from contemplating, in so many strange forms, the record of the visionaries. If we are content with the humdrum, the second-best, the hand-over-hand, it will not be forgiven us. All through the writing of this book I have been haunted by a long-remembered echo of La Princess lointaine:
>
> Brother Trophime.   Dullness is the only vice, Master Erasmus. And the only virtue is . . .
>
> Erasmus.   What?
>
> Brother Trophime.   Enthusiasm![54]

Let us now turn to the evangelicals and charismatics, who best epitomize enthusiasm.

---

[53] Richard Kroner, <u>Culture and Faith</u>, (Chicago, IL.: U. of Chicago Press, 1951), p. 135.
[54] Knox, <u>Enthusiasm</u>, pp. 590-91, translation mine. (See also p. 580).

CHAPTER TWO:  EVANGELICAL AND CHARISMATIC CHRISTIANITY

## Overview

"Have you accepted Jesus as your Lord and Savior?" (Evangelicals).

"Have you been baptized in the Holy Spirit?" (Charismatics and

Pentecostals).  Christians of these three groups share one common bond

which sets them apart from other Christians:  they have had an <u>adult</u>

conversion experience.  They may have been baptized as infants in a

mainstream denomination, but their defining moment was the instant as

<u>adults</u> when they <u>experienced</u> the Lord.  And as we shall see below,

Cursilliastas and Marriage Encountered couples may also fall into this

group.

Emotions, sermons lasting at least 30 minutes--more often an

hour  emphasis on persuasive outreach (evangelism):  all are features of

evangelical denominations and evangelical congregations within

mainstream (sometimes called mainline) Christianity.[1]  As Knox

mentioned in chapter one, people as widely diverse as Francis of Assisi

and modern revivalists all qualify.  Yes, there are important differences

between evangelicals on the one hand, and charismatics and

Pentecostals on the other.  But the overriding bond of an adult,

emotional experience reduces the impact of these differences.

---

[1] For the latter, see Ronald W. Nash (ed.), <u>Evangelical Renewal in the Mainline Church,</u> (Westchester, IL:  Crossway Books, 1988).

# Scripture Image and Implications

Evangelicals and charismatics insist that Jesus preached mainly to adults. People were leveled by their acceptance: rich and poor, educated and uneducated, worshipped together. Many responded in an emotional way; the speaking in tongues on Pentecost described by Luke in Acts 2 certainly made people think the recipients were drunk. When the Second Vatican Council inserted its famous chapter 2 "The People of God" in its Constitution on the Church, before the chapter on hierarchy and clergy, it gave a basis and firmness to the individual's dignity. Described so forcefully in I Pt 2:9-10 and Rev. 5:8-14, (and cited by Vatican II), the unstructured image of the People of God reverses and qualifies any tendency to glorify the clergy.[2] It is also a democratic principle: first come the People of God, then their leaders.

The preferred catholic image for the Church of "Body of Christ" hints that some parts of the Body are more important than other parts. "People of God" is basically equal, all sharing first an equal baptismal dignity.

COCU further elaborated the evangelical character of Christianity. Interestingly, they singled out "all people" and "individuals" as recipients of the "good news." Christians are ordained all to "a caring priesthood."[3]

Congar, who, as we noted in chapter one, insisted on the

---

[2] Abbott, Constitution on the Church, #9-10, pp. 24-27.
[3] COCU, In Quest, #8, p. 15; Consensus, III:9; VII:28.

Scriptural necessity of the Church, shocked some Catholic leaders when he also insisted that a hierarchical priesthood was consciously avoided by the early Christian Church. The Old Testament priesthood was deliberately shunned: first came the priesthood of Christ, then of the Christian faithful, and only last and late, a priestly hierarchy.[4]

## Historical Overview

Nichols felicitous expression "Evangelical Undertow" helps us understand that powerful currents of renewal exist within Christianity, bursting forth periodically and unpredictably.[5] The lay Catholic scholar Jay Dolan surprised many when he vindicated this for the parish mission within Catholicism, showing how revivals are very much a part of U.S. Catholicism.[6]

Most historians view St. Anthony and the Desert Fathers and Mothers of the third century as the first renewal.[7] The Eastern Churches, especially those in the Byzantine tradition, have institutionalized this first renewal with many feasts on their calendar. Two of the more interesting are St. Simeon Stylites (Sept. 1, beginning their Church Year) and Mary of Egypt (April 1 and Fifth Sunday of Lent).

The renewal which concerns us the most happened in the early

---

[4] Yves M.J. Congar, O.P., Lay People in the Church, (Westminster, MD: Newman Press, 1965), rev. ed., Translated by Donald Attwater, pp. 132-46.
[5] Nichols, Primer for Protestants, (NY: Association Press, 1947), pp. 34-37.
[6] Jay P. Dolan, Catholic Revivalism, (Notre Dame, IN: U. of Notre Dame Press, 1978), especially p. 186.
[7] See Laura Swan, O.S.B., The Forgotten Desert Mothers, (Mahway, NY: Paulist Press, 2001).

1700's, almost simultaneously in three places: on the Continent, especially in German Lutheranism (pietism); in the Anglican Church in England (Methodism) and in the "Great Awakening" in the American colonies (revivalism). Claude Welch and John Dillenberger, in their Protestant Christianity, link these "evangelical revivals" together because all three placed "an emphasis upon the experience of the living Christ in the hearts of men."[8]

As Catholics Knox and Merton noted in chapter one, there are always exaggerations and abuses when emotions enter into religion. Especially on the American frontier, the Methodists in particular felt these problems. The dean of Methodist church historians, William Warren Sweet wrote about the Second Awakening (late 1700's to early 1800's) and its impact on the frontier: "The revival produced several peculiar bodily exercises, such as falling, jerking, rolling, running, dancing and barking." (The barking phenomenon seems to have been limited to this revival, but we will meet the falling again in the 20th century charismatics). And Sweet concludes with an observation applicable to all evangelical bursts of fervor: "The influence of the revival upon western society was both good and evil, with good predominating."[9]

Sweet also notes that as the "popular churches" increased in prestige, the "old camp-meeting grounds" were transformed, first "into

---

[8] Claude Welch and John Dillenberger, Protestant Christianity, (NY: Scribners, 1954), p. 123).
[9] William Warren Sweet, The Story of Religion in America, (NY: Harper, 1950), p. 230. For more about barking, see his Religion on the American Frontier, The Methodists (vol. 4) (Chicago, IL: 1946).

Chautauqua assemblies and later into middle-class summer resorts." At Lake Chautauqua, near Buffalo, NY, in 1874, Methodism launched one of its greatest intellectual accomplishments. "Chautauquas" came to mean "the traveling tent companies that brought circuit programs by rail or truck or automobile to thousands of American towns and villages during the early decades of the twentieth century."[10]

From the mid-eighteenth to the early twentieth century, the American Revolution, the opening of the frontier, the coming of the machine age and the slavery question with its aftermath, confronted and occupied American Protestantism. But inside Protestantism, the tension between experience and doctrine, between those Christians emphasizing the inerrant, literal Biblical view of the world and those emphasizing the need to update and answer the challenge of an evolutionary, scientific age, was gradually building up. In the early decades of the twentieth century, the constant questioning of science finally forced Protestants to re-examine their simple Biblical view of the world. And this re-examination blew apart the American Protestant Churches. So bitter did the disputes become between fundamentalist and liberal Protestants that, in many Churches a theological depression lasted until about 1945. Because of fear of further enmity, many Protestants avoided all doctrinal discussion. (Something similar happened within Catholicism, as we

---

[10] Sweet, The Story of Religion in America, p. 346; see Theodore Morrison, Chautauqua: A Center for Education, Religion and the Arts in America (Chicago, Il: University of Chicago Press, 1974), p. vii, for the description of "Chautauquas," and pp. 173-92 for their development.

shall see in chapter four).

In the early 1940's, as the gathering war clouds brought Christians together and as time healed the wounds of past controversy, some Christians who believed in the Five Fundamentals began to rationally defend and explain these beliefs. Avoiding the label "Fundamentalists," they preferred a tag such as "Evangelical Conservatives." They still insisted on <u>experiencing</u> Christ as the basic Christian fact, but slowly they began to examine how their teachings could be more intelligible to modern people. In 1947, some of these thinkers founded Fuller Theological Seminary in Pasadena, Calif. Fuller protested the anti-intellectualism in fundamentalistic circles, the detachment from social issues and the tendency to shatter the traditional churches into smaller denominations. High academic standards and social concern slowly reinforced the basic evangelical experience.

It was also in 1947 that Carl Henry, perhaps the leading thinker of this moderate group, published <u>The Uneasy Conscience of Modern Fundamentalism</u>[11] and set the review <u>Christianity Today</u>[12] on its feet as the consistent voice of this new movement. All through the 1950's, in the Protestant Churches from Baptist through Episcopalian, those Christians who called themselves "Evangelical" continued to grow in numbers and influence.

---

[11] Carl F.H. Henry, <u>The Uneasy Conscience of Modern Fundamentalism</u>, (Grand Rapids, MI: Eerdmans, 1947).
[12] <u>Christianity Today</u> describes itself as "founded by Billy Graham."

Moreover, those denominations where evangelicals were in the clear majority, such as the Southern Baptist Convention, grew at a remarkable pace. The election of Southern Baptist Jimmy Carter as president of the United States in 1976 brought new respectability to evangelicals. In 1962 Southern Baptists replaced Methodists as the largest single Protestant denomination in the USA.[13] And Dean Kelley's work Why the Conservative Churches Are Growing caught the attention of many Christians in the English speaking world.[14]

Also attention getting was the growing divide; Methodist Thomas Oden snapped "Precious little attempt has been made to reach out for the liberal denominations' nearest neighbors in the ecumenical village: their own evangelical counterparts."[15]

In 1980, the Jesuit Thomas Clancy provided an easily accessible survey of both the blurring, and the growing difference between evangelicals and fundamentalists: "Fundamental Facts About Evangelicals." By this time, he found that "An Evangelical has been defined as a noncantankerous Fundamentalist," with Billy Graham the former and Bob Jones the latter.[16]

---

[13] The Methodist Church, 10,153,003 (for 1962, p. 257); the Southern Baptist Convention, 10,191,303 (for 1962, p. 254): Yearbook of American Churches, ed. Benson Y. Landis (New York: National Council of Churches, 1964).

[14] Dean Kelley, Why The Conservative Churches Are Growing, (NY: Harper, 1972).

[15] Thomas Oden, Requiem: A Lament in Three Movements, (Nashville, TN: Abingdon, 1995), p. 93.

[16] Thomas Clancy, S.J., "Fundamental Facts About Evangelicals," America, May 31, 1980, pp. 454-57.

# Charismatic Emergence

During the night of February 17-18, 1967, several Duquesne University (Pittsburgh, PA) students and recent graduates took a break from a party to pray in the chapel, during a retreat. They received what they and 13 others soon recognized as baptism in the Holy Spirit. Jim Manney, editor of the New Covenant magazine observed in 1992:

> None of them thought they were starting a renewal movement. Yet within three years the Catholic charismatic renewal had an international conference, publishing houses, a magazine, a tape and book ministry, must-read books, theological advisers, hundreds of prayer groups in North America and Europe, and a pastoral oversight committee with links to the conference of U.S. bishops and Rome.[17]

At about the same time, this phenomenon burst out in Protestant and Orthodox Churches all over the world. First known as the Catholic Pentecostal Movement (some early books used that expression), it soon became recognized in practically all denominations as the charismatic movement. During September 1970-December 1974 I was able to closely observe its growth each Friday evening at Catholic University of America, Washington, DC. From 1975 to June, 2001, I followed it at Our Lady of Hope Charismatic Center, Newburgh, NY. There is no doubt that the core group (those who have undergone the "Life in the Spirit Seminar" and subsequent Baptism in the Holy Spirit) represent but a fraction of those who attend.

---

[17] Jim Manney, "The People's Movement at Age 25," New Covenant, July 1996, p. 16. Fr. Michael Scanlan calls this article "my favorite" of all the articles in the 25 years of New Covenant (ibid.).

Jim Manney observed in 1992:

> It became the biggest grassroots movement in
> Catholicism in years, perhaps since the Franciscan renewal
> of the 13th century. Other Catholic renewal movements--
> Cursillo, Catholic Action, Catholic Worker, the Catholic
> Family Movement and movements to renew worship and to
> promote Scripture reading--had specialized purposes and
> were usually confined to a small group of activists and
> intellectuals.[18]

I remember taking one well read and energetic Oblate priest to the

Catholic University prayer group. When the young man next to us raised

his hands over his head and began speaking in tongues, my companion

had all he could do to avoid walking out.

For Catholics, the Constitution on the Liturgy of Vatican II enabled

charismatics to develop the distinctive evangelical prayer style within the

Catholic Mass. Rejecting "rigid uniformity" there was now room within

the structure of the Mass for personal testimony by individuals,

spontaneous praise, and a much fuller use of Scripture.[19] The abolition

of Latin, which the Council began, was the necessary prerequisite.

At the same time, Afro-American Catholics, and Hispanic

Catholics, were developing worship very different in style from the pre-

Vatican II Latin Mass. This too aided charismatics to pursue a worship

style with resemblances to evangelical Protestant worship.

The presence of observers from the Eastern Orthodox Churches at

the Vatican Council enabled the tiny percentage of Council Fathers

---

[18] Manney, New Covenant, July 1996, p. 16.
[19] See for example, Abbott, Constitution on the Liturgy, #'s 24, 34, 35 and expecially 37 (pp. 147-51).

familiar with Eastern Theology to insert references to the Holy Spirit in the documents (although after the basic texts were written). A theology of the Holy Spirit joined the gifts present in charismatic worship, enabling a liturgy truly emotional and Spirit based.

The Presbyterian Worshipbook of 1970 opened the way for evangelical/charismatic worship within the Presbyterian/Reformed tradition. A little noted rubric permitted testimony during official Sunday worship, something which catholic Presbyterian liturgists had avoided in earlier worship books.[20]

Having Mass celebrated in homes became something of a practice immediately after Vatican II. Now groups such as Marriage Encounter and Cursillo were joined by charismatics in developing worship which was adapted to the goals of their group. It became evident that many of the charismatics came from the earlier renewal groups. The emergence of the charismatic movement strengthened the more adapted style of worship of other renewal groups, and represented a convergence of all Christians who received an adult conversion experience. By the end of the century, the Vatican noticed this and began meetings to bring the various renewal groups together (see below).

---

[20] United Presbyterian Church USA, The Worshipbook (Philadelphia, PA: Westminster Press, 1970), p. 28, and continued in Book of Common Worship (Louisville, KY: Westminster/John Knox Press, 1993), p. 63. See Harry E. Winter O.M.I., "Presbyterians Pioneer the Vatican II Sunday Lectionary," Journal of Ecumenical Studies, 38 (Spring-Summer, 2001, #2-3): 142-43.

## Charismatics and Classical Pentecostals

As the charismatic movement grew in the 1970's, many religious leaders wondered if it would converge with the classical Pentecostal and Holiness Churches of the early 1900's. These groups grew out of the lower economic and social classes of the USA. Speaking in tongues and baptism in the Spirit made them unwelcome in more traditional Protestant Churches.

The convergence did occur: Gros calls the international Pentecostal-Catholic dialogue of the last three decades "astonishing."[21] The same convergence has happened in World Council of Churches circles: the first international dialogue between a worldwide family of Protestant Churches and the Pentecostal Movement occurred in July, 1995.[22]

When the revered Presbyterian leader John Mackay visited Latin America, he declared, "The future of the Gospel in Latin America is in the hands of the Roman Catholics and the Pentecostals."[23] And by Catholics, he meant especially charismatics, who adhered to Vatican II's work on the essential role of the Bible, continual reform, devotion to a renewed papacy, etc.

Nor is it coincidental that George MacLeod, founder of the Iona

---

[21] Gros, Intro. To Ecumenism, p. 228; see pp. 24, 227-30.
[22] Frank D. Macchia, "Spirit, Word and Kingdom: Theological Reflections on the Reformed/Pentecostal Dialogue", Ecumenical Trends 30 (March 2001, #3): 1/33-7/39.
[23] W. Dayton Roberts, "Latin American Charismatics Are Here to Stay," Latin America Evangelist, March-April 1977, p. 10.

Community mentioned in chapter one, became very much a charismatic figure forward the end of his life, urging Presbyterians and all Christians to be open to this group.[24]

Let there be no mistake: there are still Christians who call themselves evangelical, but exude a fundamentalistic fear of anything Catholic or catholic. There are still Pentecostals who would not be caught dead with a Catholic or an Eastern Orthodox Christian. But more and more there is a remarkable convergence of Pentecostals, evangelicals and charismatics.

## Further Developments within Evangelicalism

The technique of outreach called revivals or evangelism has increasingly joined all these groups. Billy Graham's "Crusades" led the way. Graham made it an early practice to refer those raised in a different Christian Church, back to that Church before he would accept them. For this, Bob Jones told him he was not welcome at fundamentalistic Bob Jones University.[25]

Graham's 11 times a year magazine Decision is well done, and seems to go out of its way to reach all Christians, without proselytizing.[26]

Gros has observed: "Catholics have a long history of collaboration with evangelicals in outreach to the unchurched, as in the Billy Graham

---

[24] New Covenant, Presbyterian-Charismatic Conference, June, 1973, p. 7, text 10-12.
[25] See for example Rausch, America, May 31, 1980, p. 454.
[26] Decision, begun in 1959, available from Billy Graham Evangelistic Association, 1300 Harmon Place, P.O. Box 779, Minneapolis, NM 55440.

Crusades," and he cites Boston, Massachusetts, 1964 as the first.[27]

Noteworthy also was the effort in Texas, "Good News Texas" by Southern Baptists (1977),[28] and "A National Festival of Evangelism" (1988).[29]  Recently, the Alpha Model has energized many denominations, growing, for example, in the Catholic  Church from 5 courses in 1992, to 2,500 in 1995, to 16,150 in 2000 (world-wide).[30]

Now, Catholic charismatics (and charismatics from all Churches) are joining with evangelicals and Pentecostals in evangelizing.  And the structures of all denominations are being affected; the fact that Neuhaus could make the suggestion on the floor of the synod of bishops concerning joint Catholic and evangelical evangelization of the Americas shows those structures slowly being permeated by an evangelical ecumenism.

Charismatics and evangelicals are moved by their adult conversion experience to witness first of all <u>one-on-one</u>.  This instinctive response was described many years ago by the celebrated Indian Methodist D.T. Niles.  He defined evangelism as "one beggar telling another beggar where to find bread."[31]  Note how this approach goes directly to the individual,

---

[27] Gros, "Evangelical Relations", <u>Ecumenical Trends</u> 29, (Jan. 2000, #1):7.  The 9 page article is excellent.

[28] See section 2 below for cooperation with Catholics.

[29] "Ecumenical Cooperation," <u>Ecumenical Trends</u> 15, (April, 1986, #4): 62-63.

[30] See CHRISTLIFE:  Catholic Evangelization Services, 12290-A Folly Quarter Road, Ellicott City, Maryland 21042, USA.

[31] See James B. Simpson, <u>Simpson's Contemporary Quotations,</u> (Houghton Mifflin Co., 1988), #4239, attributed to D.T. Niles in <u>NY Times,</u> May 11, 1986.  A slightly different version is cited in J. Robert Nelson, "Ecumenical Prophets and Pioneers: D.T. Niles," <u>Ecumenical Trends</u> 9 (July/Aug. 1980, #7):  102.

obscuring the place of society, which COCU and Pope Paul VI emphasized (see above, ch. 1). But it has the advantage of energetic directness.

In 1974, two events further emphasized the growing difference between evangelicals stressing an adult conversion experience, and fundamentalists stressing stability around incontestable doctrine. Richard Quebedeaux published his The Young Evangelicals, and "The Lausanne Covenant" was produced as a mission statement.

Quebedeaux's book, subtitled "Revolution in Orthodoxy," documented and pleaded for further repudiation of "the theological and cultural excesses of Fundamentalism."[32] "The Lausanne Covenant," with Billy Graham as its chief inspirer and Anglican Scripture scholar John R.W. Stott[33] as a framer, signaled a move away from fundamentalism's fear and bitterness towards other Christians, to a need for cooperation. And the evangelical emphasis on individual action was balanced by a concern to work for social justice changing unjust and oppressive government and economic policies.[34]

Campus Crusade for Christ continued to grow in its effectiveness on college and university campuses. Time Magazine credited its founder Bill Bright with a major role in the Jesus Movement of the early 1970's,

---

[32] Richard Quebedeaux, The Young Evangelicals, (NY: Harper, 1974), p. 3; for the growing popularity of Niles definition, p. 89.
[33] See his Christian Mission in the Modern World (Downers Grove, IL, 1975, InterVarsity Press).
[34] Originally published in Christianity Today, see John R.W. Stott (ed), Making Christ Known: Historic Mission Documents from the Lausanne Movement, 1974-89 (Grand Rapids, MI: Eerdmans 1997).

dedicating the cover of its June 21, 1971 issue to Jesus.[35] Campus

Crusade's tri-annual Christmas vacation convention by 2000 drew over

18,000 delegates to the University of Illinois' Urbana campus. Advertised

by the InterVarsity Christian Fellowship as a foreign missions gathering,

it was also drawing observers from non-evangelical groups.[36]

But the earliest evangelical group to document for its maturing is

World Vision. Many of its workers in predominantly Catholic countries

are now Catholics. Cooperative ventures abound. And its newest

journal, Global Future, continues to demonstrate the move from

individual solutions to also working with governments and other religions

to effect structural change.[37]

The leader of the growing number of Catholic bishops to reach out

to World Vision is Ricardo Ramirez of Las Cruces, NM. His presentation

to the World Vision Partnership Ministry Team Meeting, Seattle,

Washington in Feb. 1996 is readily accessible.[38]

As Quebedeaux demonstrated in Young Evangelicals, politics is no

longer taboo for evangelicals. The Christian Coalition and TV evangelist

Pat Robertson joined forces especially in the 1988 presidential primary.[39]

By 1979, evangelicals and Catholics were officially dialoguing.

---

[35] Time Magazine, June 21, 1971, especially pp. 56-63.

[36] "Urbana 2000," American Bible Society Record, April/May 2001, pp. 16-17.

[37] World Vision, Global Future, Fourth Quarter, 2000 (1st number), quarterly.

[38] Ricardo Ramirez, C.S.B., "Towards a More Perfect Union," Ecumenical Trends 25 (Nov. 1996, #10): 11/155-16/160, especially his explanation of "Mainline Evangelical groups in Latin America" (p. 13/157).

[39] Quebedeaux, Young Evangelicals, pp. 118-35; for Pat Robertson, see ch. 4 below..

Catholic press noted, "The First National Convocation of Christian Leaders bringing Catholic and evangelical leaders together was attended by 800 leaders. As recently as five years ago, these two elements of Christianity were seen not only as incompatible but contradictory."[40] (The convocation was held at Stanford University, California, Aug. 27-31, 1979).

Southern Baptist-Catholic cooperation peaked in the early 1980's, and then declined until the new millennium. The death of SB Dr. Carlyle Marney in 1978 removed a voice which was heard at Presbyterian and Methodist seminaries, one which pastors of every denomination listened to intently. His "Interpreters' House" at Lake Junaluska, NC was not exactly a haven but more a hospital. "I have no hope that you won't bleed. I have a hope that you won't bleed unnecessarily, unworthily and fatally."[41]

A truly extraordinary team of SB Dr. C.B. Hastings and Catholic Fr. Joe O'Donnell (Glenmary Missionary) had brought many Catholic parishes and SB congregations closer together in the 1970's. However, Hastings retired from his post as "Staff Member in the Department of Interfaith Witness of the S.B. Home Mission Board" (R.C., Eastern Orthodox, etc.) and almost simultaneously O'Donnell retired from his position as "liaison (or field representative) to Southern Baptists for the

---

[40] NC news release, Catholic Virginian, Sept. 10, 1979, p. 8.
[41] Marney, quoted by William H. Willimon, "A Prophet Leaves Us: Carlyle Marney," Christian Century, July 19-26, 1978, p. 695. For more on Marney, see David Stricklin, A Geneology of Dissent (Lexington, KY: University Press of Kentucky, 1999).

Bishops' Committee on Ecumenical and Inter-religious Affairs." For reasons not entirely evident today, the SB Convention then started splitting between moderates and fundamentalists. Growth slowed, and in 1998, the first loss in 72 years occurred, down 1% to 15.7 million members.[42] Bill Broadway, writing in the Washington Post, noted in October, 2000 that "an increasing number of congregations have withdrawn their Southern Baptist Convention affiliation in recent months. . . . Some have chosen to remain independent, often dropping 'Baptist' from their names, while others have affiliated with American Baptists, National Baptists, Progressive National Baptists or a combination."[43]

In 2000, the most famous SB of all, former president Jimmy Carter withdrew because of the "increasingly rigid" stand of the denomination.[44]

But in April 2001, Associated Press noted that SBC membership "climbed to record levels in 2000, reaching nearly 16 million despite internal controversies over the church's heightened conservatism and fundamentalist views."[45]

The cooperation between SBC and other Christians in the bell-weather state of Texas, which had been so promising in the 1970's, revived in 2000. In February and October, leaders of the Texas Conference of Churches (which includes Catholic and Greek Orthodox,

---

[42] Associated Press, Evening Sun (Norwich, NY), April 30, 1999, p. 17.
[43] Bill Broadway, Washington Post byline, Buffalo News, Oct. 29, 2000, p. A-3.
[44] Kristen Wyatt, AP article, Buffalo News, Oct. 21, 2000, p. A-11.
[45] AP release, Evening Sun (Norwich, NY), April 27, 2000, p. 10.

also) met with leaders of the Baptist General Convention of Texas.[46]

They resolved to include worship and Bible study in future meetings.

And the first of "the three most pressing concerns for the Baptists of

Texas" is the perception "that half of the population of Texas does not

attend church."[47]

Other evangelical groups also moved towards cooperation. The

National Association of Evangelicals (NAE) decided to admit

denominations that affirm evangelical principles even if they also hold

membership in the National Council of Churches. The Reformed Church

in America, a charter member of the NCC, was the agent of change.[48]

There was some backlash, which culminated in the resignation of NAE's

president, Rev. Kevin Mannoia.[49]

The epoch making 1994 statement "Evangelicals and Catholics

Together: The Christian Mission in the Third Millennium" (ECT) further

revealed which evangelicals wanted to work with other Christians,

especially Catholics, and which were fundamentalist at heart.[50] A great

deal of controversy accompanied the evangelical signers;[51] at first,

Catholics tended to ignore ECT. Gros called the Catholic response

---

[46] Terry L. White, "Texas Conference of Churches Meets with Texas Baptists," Texas Ecumenical Action, Oct. 2000 (46, #4), pp. 1-2.
[47] Ibid. p. 1.
[48] Associated Press, Evening Sun (Norwich, NY), March 17, 2000, p. 9.
[49] Associated Press, Evening Sun, June 29, 2001, p. 11.
[50] Text first published in First Things, 1994, (May, #43): 15-22.
[51] Rausch summarizes this very well: "Catholics and Evangelicals in Dialogue, "A Catholic Perspective," Ecumenical Trends 30 (Jan. 2001, p. 7-12), with excellent documentation.

"minimal and mostly positive."[52]  When the Vatican came on board,

Catholics and observers from many denominations began to suspect that

something new was afoot:  convergence was reaching new levels.

Perhaps the most interesting article in the noteworthy achievement of six

authors concerning ECT is J.I. Packer's "Crosscurrents among

Evangelicals."[53]  Until the final paragraph, one is not sure that Packer is

subscribing to ECT.  Also noteworthy is Dulles' contribution "The Unity

for Which We Hope"; he gives very concrete and realistic

recommendations for joint work, "a ten-point program."[54]  Also

significant is that all three evangelicals document the growing

convergence of evangelicals and charismatics.

Perhaps the most succinct statement of ECT concerns evangelism:

"As Christ is one, so the Christian mission is one.  The one mission can

be and should be advanced in diverse ways."[55]  Rausch gives an excellent

survey of ECT developments through 1999, including mentioning the

work of Bishop Ramirez, and Allan Figueroa Deck (both Hispanic

Catholics).[56]

C.S. Lewis probably smiled when two of the supporters of ECT took

a leading role in a conference held in the summer of 1998 at Seattle

---

[52] Jeff Gros PSC., "Evangelical Relations," Ecumenical Trends 29 (Jan. 2000, #1), p. 4.

[53] J.I. Packer, "Crosscurrents Among Evangelicals," Evangelicals and Catholics:  Toward A Common Mission (Dallas, TX:  Word Publishing, 1995), Charles Colson and Richard Neuhaus, ed., pp. 147-74.

[54] Avery Dulles, S.J., "The Unity for Which We Hope," ibid., pp. 115-46, especially 138-40.

[55] ECT, First Things, p. 15; also in Colson and Neuhaus, p. xv.

[56] Thomas P. Rausch S.J., "Catholic and Evangelicals in Dialogue:  A Catholic Perspective," Ecumenical Trends 30 (Jan. 2001, #1): pp. 7-12, with thorough bibliography.

Pacific University and Seattle's First Free Methodist Church to commemorate Lewis's birthday centennial. Peter Kreeft (Catholic) and Kent Hill (Nazarene) dialogued on Lewis' impact on both evangelicals and Catholics.[57] Much of the report centered on ECT's continuing influence.

The evolution of the evangelical American Bible Society towards Catholic and Eastern Orthodox is also clear. Until Vatican II revealed Catholic interest in the Bible, ABS literature spoke only of <u>converting</u> Catholics and Orthodox. By 2001, ABS produced the Good News Bible including "the complete Roman Catholic Lectionary Guide," a Catholic priest served on staff, and a web site included articles "on how Catholics and Pentecostals can come to a better understanding of their different Christian traditions."[58] For a positive view of the Eastern Orthodox, see David Singer, "Easter Is Coming In the Middle East."[59] A $4.00 annual contribution will bring six issues a year of a magazine remarkable for its ability to appeal to all five models.[60]

The increasing convergence of evangelicals and Catholics is symbolized by the "Consultation" (less formal than a dialogue) between the World Evangelical Fellowship and the Vatican. The first took place in 1993, the second in 1997, the third in 1999, and the fourth in 2001, on

---

[57] Beth Grubb, "Scholars reflect on legacy of C.S. Lewis," <u>Catholic NW Progress</u>, Sept. 3, 1998, pp. 3, 19.

[58] Peter Feuerherd, FORMINISTRY.COM," <u>American Bible Society Record</u>, Dec. 2000 (146, #1), p. 10.

[59] David Singer, "Easter Is Coming In the Middle East," <u>American Bible Society Record</u>, April 1999 (144, #3), pp. 4-6.

[60] ABS Record, 1865 Broadway, NY 10023.

three different continents.[61]

A more formal "dialogue" did occur between "some Lausanne Committee leaders, convened by the Anglican John Stott" and "Catholic theologians and missiologists named by the Vatican." Three meetings produced "the honest 1986 Report which still remains ground breaking: The Evangelical-Roman Catholic Dialogue on Mission 1977-84 [ERCDOM]."[62]

## Charismatic and Pentecostal Developments

Father Kilian McDonnell, the foremost Catholic scholar on both the Pentecostal and Charismatic movements, took the opportunity of Harvey Cox's 1994 book on classic Pentecostalism Fire From Heaven[63] to write a thorough study on the Pentecostal-Catholic Dialogue. In one of the longest articles every published in America, he examined how the charismatic movement was part of the "Classical Pentecostal/Roman Catholic Dialogue." He quotes approvingly Cardinal Dulles remark that the "evangelical turn in the ecclesial vision of Popes Paul VI and John Paul II is one of the most surprising and important developments in the Catholic Church since Vatican II."[64] Now Pentecostals and charismatics started evangelizing together, first side by side and then increasingly as

---

[61] "Communique," Ecumenical Trends 29 (March, 2000, #3): 15/47-16/48 (first three); fourth, Ecumenical Trends 30 (Nov. 2001, #10): 3/147.

[62] Thomas F. Stransky, C.S.P., "A Catholic Looks at Evangelical Protestants," Priests and People, Jan. 1998 (12; #1), p. 7.

[63] Harvey Cox, Fire From Heaven (Reading, MA: Addison-Wesley, 1995).

[64] Kilian McDonnell, O.S.B, "The Death of Mythologies," America, March 25, 1995, p. 15 (14-19).

one.

The July 8-14, 1991 International Charismatic Consultation on World Evangelization helped charismatics to see the value of ecumenism.[65]

In the mid-1990's some of the more promising Catholic charismatic groups suffered a great deal from problems typical to enthusiastic revivals. The Gaithersburg, MD "Mother of God Community," which had a perceptive and prolific priest-writer as part of its leadership, English born Peter Hocken, was directed to reform itself by the Archdiocese of Washington. The Washington Post thoroughly documented the effort in two lengthy articles.[66]

The "Mother of God Community" founded an excellent Scripture magazine, The Word Among Us, (eleven times a year in English, six in Spanish). It suffered a temporary decline, but seems to have recovered its poise. Circulation was 173,000 in 1993, dropped to 160,000 in 1995, and rebounded to 230,000 by 2002.[67]

Since the Memorial Day Weekend of 1995 drew over 52,000 men to the Promise Keepers Rally in Washington, DC May 27-29, The Washington Post gave much space to this phenomenon, which attracted

---

[65] Raniero Cantalamessa, O.F.M., "That they may all be one so that the world may believe," One in Christ 27 (1991, #3): 201-08.

[66] Justin Gillis, "In the Name of God," Washington Post Magazine, April 13, 1997, pp. 13-31; "Paradise Lost," April 20, 1997, pp. 15-31.

[67] Correspondence and phone calls, June 24, 2002 to Oct. 4, 2002, Mother of God Community File.

especially evangelicals and charismatics.[68]  For the first weekend, in Oct., 1997, national rally, <u>Time Magazine</u> devoted their cover and feature story to the movement.[69]

The National Conference of Catholic Bishops held a two day consultation "with about twenty leaders from this mushrooming movement" in Sept . 1998.  Its report "Catholic Men's Ministries" shows a varied approach to the oversight of Catholics in this movement.[70]  A more cautionary article appeared by Fr. Walter Woods in <u>America</u>.[71]

## Ethical Issues:  Abortion, Capital Punishment, Abstinence

The abortion issue especially drew many evangelicals to cooperate with Catholics and catholics within ecumenical Christianity.  George A. Wesolek, executive director of the Justice and Peace Commission for the Catholic  Archdiocese of San Francisco, examined this perceptively, joining "family life, euthanasia (right to die laws) and sexuality with all their murky public policy nuances" to abortion as issues where evangelicals and Catholics are converging.[72]

Perhaps two-thirds of evangelicals (and catholics) are in favor of capital punishment.  A widely circulated video made the case for capital

---

[68] Laurie Goodstein, <u>Washington Post</u>, May 28, 1995, pp. A-1, A-6,7.

[69] <u>Time Magazine</u>, October 6, 1997.

[70] Committee on Marriage and Family, Committee on Evangelization, National Conference of Catholic Bishops, <u>Catholic Men's Ministries:  An Introductory Report</u>, July, 1999, 11 pp.

[71] Walter J. Woods, "Promise Keepers:  How Should Catholics Respond?," <u>America</u>, Dec. 13, 1997, pp. 18-20.

[72] George A. Wesolek, "A New Reality--A New Alliance," <u>America</u>, Nov. 9, 1991, pp. 340-41. He explores very well the tension with liberals.

punishment very strongly from the issue of justice as necessary before

mercy, considering a sophisticated argument from Scripture.[73]

However, voices did begin to emerge within the evangelical

community differing over the death penalty. The American Bible

Society's Record documented the difference between SBC's Dr. Richard

Land (for the death penalty) and Huntsville, TX (where Texas houses its

death row) pastor Ken Hugghins (against).[74]

The abstinence pledge (from sexual intercourse before marriage)

originated with S. Baptist teens; it quickly spread to Catholic circles, and

government programs.[75]

The best place to see how these ethical issues play out is the 10

times a year American Family Association Journal. Slick, sophisticated,

and based on a growing number of state affiliates, it seeks to monitor

and influence legislation affecting many legal issues: pornography,

media influence, homosexuality, gambling, etc. It was the first to

publicize the bias in the media treatment of the murder of the 13-year

old boy in Arkansas by two gays.[76]

---

[73] Richard Maler, 4138 S. 3rd St., Milwaukee, WI 53207, mailing to seminaries especially, the video by Pastor Arnold Murray, tape 410, Capital Punishment.

[74] ABS Record, "Bible in the News," Dec. 2000/Jan. 2001, p. 21.

[75] See for example the NY State government abstinence initiative described as including Buffalo Catholic Charities, WNY Catholic, July, 1999, p. 14.

[76] American Family Association Journal, May 2001, p. 4 (P.O. Drawer 2440, Tupelo, MS 38803), ABC National Evening News treatment of this episode, April 2001 seemed particularly defensive in nature, and offensive to many people.

## Evangelical Culture and Spirituality

The repentant slave trader John Newton's hymn "Amazing Grace" captures the ethos of evangelicals, charismatics and Pentecostals. Richard R. Gilbert noted "the pious subjectivity so despised by modern hymnologists is perfectly captured with 'now I see.'"[77] Then Gilbert continues by praising the relevancy of the hymn.

The "we" which catholics insist upon in worship needs to be balanced by the "I" (I believe, I testify). Because the born again and baptized in the Spirit experiences happen to <u>individuals</u>, evangelicals and charismatics insist on "I" language in worship.

As the 1990's progressed, travelers in Pennsylvania, Maryland, Virginia and West Virginia noticed three crosses illuminated at night, gracing many hilltops. A Methodist lay leader and oil driller, Bernard Coffindaffer took it as his mission to buy or lease land and erect these crosses. His first goal was to place them near every court house; then he expanded.[78] Catholics have their style of affecting culture; Coffindaffer's is a typical evangelical effort.

First in the teen culture, then it seemed everywhere, appeared the initials WWJD: "What would Jesus Do?" One Catholic youth expert, Tom Beaudoin, observed "we have much to learn from our evangelical

---

[77] Richard R. Gilbert, "'Amazing Grace': Past and Present," <u>Presbyterian Life</u>, Feb. 1, 1970, pp. 36-37.

[78] Marc Fisher, "Coffindaffer's Crosses," <u>Washington Post Magazine</u>, Feb. 22, 1987, pp. 16-23; 44-45. See also the <u>Charleston (WV) Gazette</u>, Phil Kabler, "Coffindaffer Profiled in Magazine," Feb. 24, 1987, p. 12A.

brothers and sisters." Then he went on to express catholic reservations

about "reductionism."[79]

Quebedeaux claimed C.S. Lewis and Dietrich Bonhoeffer as

"intellectual roots" of evangelicalism's growth.[80] The literature on its

spirituality is immense. Perhaps the best classic is Hannah Hurnard's

Hinds Feet on High Places.[81]

As the phenomenon of home schooling grew, Washington Post

writer Peter Y. Hong noted "about 80% of parents nationwide who teach

their children at home are conservative Christians."[82]

Among evangelical think tanks, the Moody Institute has a long

history of achievement. A Jesuit reviewer, Dennis R. Parnell quoted

approvingly Edward Larson's statement "Scientific observation revealed a

conspicuous design in nature that could only be explained by a religion

and a creator God." Parnell then commented "Such was the message of

the films of the Moody Institute of Science, which were shown to U.S.

servicemen as part of their basic training until the 1960's."[83]

A charismatic Catholic loaned me the three videotape series The

Wonder of God's Creation, a more recent development by the Moody

[79] Tom Beaudoin, "A Peculiar Contortion," America, Sept. 18, 1999, pp. 16-19.

[80] Quebedeaux, Young Evangelicals, pp. 61-68.

[81] Hannah Hurnard, Hinds Feet on High Places, (Tyndale, 1955). Her later book, Eagle's Wings, was accused of being pantheistic.

[82] Peter Y. Hong, "Home-Schooled Christian Teens Tout Advantages of Their Lifestyle," Washington Post, Oct. 16, 1994, B3.

[83] Dennis R. Parnell, S.J., "Book Reviews," Summer for the Gods, by Edward J. Larson (Basic Books, 1998), in America, May 2, 1998, pp. 23-24.

Institute. The beauty and sophistication of these videos is remarkable.[84]

## As the Millennium Begins

A rather breathless article appeared in The Atlantic Monthly "The Opening of the Evangelical Mind." Written by an author who would probably describe himself as liberal, for a liberal audience, the article is a comprehensive survey of Evangelicalism. [85]

In India, Charismatics influenced the Eastern Oriental Syro-Malabar Church. Pentecostal missionaries also are credited with inspiring this renewal.[86]

In the USA, charismatic influence probably had declined slightly. Bernard Lee S.M., in his Lilly Endowment funded study of Small Church Communities (in the Catholic Church), estimated that of 37,000 identifiable small Christian communities, 4,800 are charismatic--still a significant number.[87]

Rather than decline, some would call it institutionalization. Certainly the FIRE program (Faith, Intercession, Repentance and Evangelism) is growing. A rally in Buffalo, NY drew about 2,700

---

[84] The Moody Institute of Science, Chicago, IL. 60610, The Wonder of God's Creation, three videos.

[85] Alan Wolfe, "The Opening of the Evangelical Mind," The Atlantic Monthly, October 2000, pp. 55-76.

[86] Sean Sprague, "The Church Is A-Changing," Catholic Near East 26 (July-Aug. 2000, #4): 22-25. This very readable magazine is now called CNEWA World (Catholic Near East Welfare Association) and is published six times a year.

[87] See the analysis by Robert K. Moriarty S.M., "Parish and Small Church Communities," America, May 7, 2001, pp. 14-19. Lee's book is The Catholic Experience of Small Christian Communities (Mahwah, NY: Paulist, 2000.

participants, with Buffalo's daily paper headlining the event: "Catholic evangelical rally has the fire of a revival meeting."[88]

But Southern Baptists continued to split. Second Baptist Church of Libery, MO, "one of the original members of the Southern Baptist Convention, has left the denomination, which it thinks has become too restrictive in its theology," was the way Knight Ridder Newspaper's reporter Helen T. Gray put it.[89]

Associated Press writer Richard Ostling viewed the August, 2000 Netherlands conference as the 3rd of evangelical mission meetings, continuing Lausanne of 1974 and Amsterdam of 1983. Although Billy Graham did not attend, his moderating influence was strongly felt.[90]

Associated Press writer Roger Alford felt that Graham's mantle, at least for small towns sometimes bypassed, had fallen on Rick Gage. Alford noted that Gage has led more than 500 small-town crusades very successfully.[91]

The Vatican showed concern for the abuses of charismatic healing ministry, organizing a conference November 10-13, 2001 on the outskirts of Rome. John Thavis, of Catholic News Service, felt "charismatics have found a cautious ally in U.S. Cardinal J. Francis Stafford . . . who thinks healing ministry should be promoted in the church" as one of the new

---

[88] Julie Loft and Dan Herbeck, Buffalo News, Sept. 17, 2000, p. B-3.
[89] Helen T. Gray, "Church is latest to quit Southern Baptist Ranks," Buffalo News, May 19, 2001, p. A-7.
[90] Richard N. Ostling, "World Evangelical rally ends Sunday," Buffalo News, August 5, 2000.
[91] Roger Alford, "Evangelist focuses on towns bypassed by Billy Graham and others," Evening Sun (Norwich, NY), Nov. 22, 2001, p. 13.

forms of evangelization pushed by John Paul II.[92]

When one remembers that some Catholic renewal groups, such as Focolare and the Community of San Egidio, and Presbyterian groups such as Taize and Iona, are strongly sympathetic to the emotionalism of evangelicals, the new millennium began with a pattern of convergence. Many catholic groups, such as the Legion of Mary began to join with charismatic and evangelical groups to jointly evangelize. FIRE and Alpha showed that evangelism attracted catholics, too. Social justice issues such as abortion found the two models working together, also. By February, 2001, representatives of the charismatic movement were joined in Rome by Focolare's Chiara Lubich, San Egidio's Andrea Riccardi, Cursillo, International Center of Communion and Liberation, and Legionaries of Christ leaders, representing 70 million Christians world-wide. They met to "discuss how to show Christian love to the world,"[93]

I am indebted to Jeff Smith, editor of The Word Among Us, for the observation that the permanent deaconate of the Catholic Church in the USA has been heavily influenced by the charismatic movement.[94] This means that people trained in the sacramental and institutional way (catholic) are now showing the influence of the charismatic/evangelical

---

[92] John Thavis, "Pastoral Crossroads: Vatican Discusses Healing with Charismatics," The Catholic Northwest Progress, Nov. 22, 2001, p. 13.

[93] National Catholic Register, Feb. 25-March 3, 2001, p. 4. Earlier, April 28-May 1, 2000, many of these groups met in Rimini, Italy: National Catholic Register, May 7-13, 2000, p. 4.

[94] Jeff Smith to Harry Winter, Oct. 4, 2002, Mother of God Community file.

way.

From April 11-13, 2002, a very important meeting of evangelical and Catholic leaders took place at Wheaton College. New levels of trust, friendship and candor were achieved.[95]

However, evangelicalism's lack of concern for the institutional church may be spreading to the charismatic groups. Marsden observes that for evangelicals, "even the local congregation, while extremely important for fellowship purposes, is often regarded as a convenience for the individual."[96] Whether the catholic sense of the church's importance across time and space prevails, or whether the evangelical/charismatic's emphasis on the importance of the individual overcomes it, seems to be a matter of local leadership and oversight.

The way which grew out of a desire to bridge differences certainly has some role in the above convergence and tension. But how large a role did neo-orthodox/Vatican II Christians play? Let us now turn to that way.

---

[95] Thomas P. Rausch, S.J., "Another Step Forward," America, July 15-22, 2002, pp. 7-9.
[96] George M. Marsden, Understanding Fundamentalism and Evangelicalism (Grand Rapids, MI: Eerdmans, 1991), p. 81.

# Chapter Three: Neo-Orthodox Protestantism and Vatican II Catholicism: The Reformed

## Overview

During the last half of the twentieth century, a Protestant and a Catholic impulse at renewal converged, to form a powerful model for all Christians: The Reformed. Of course, this model had been present since the earliest days of Christianity. But during the 1950-2000 period, several historical factors made it especially powerful, although it had begun to wane even before the year 2000. However, it is far from dead. The tragedy of September 11, 2001 may have revived the reformed impulse, even as it was originally amplified by World War II.

Historians have dubbed the Protestant impulse "Neo-orthodoxy," since it sought to recover the orthodoxy of the original Protestant reformers such as Martin Luther and John Calvin. The Catholic impulse at reform during Vatican II quickly attracted the attention of the neo-Orthodox, and Catholics themselves began to again use the term "Reformers." Tracy, for example, has no hesitation in speaking of "Catholic theological neo-orthodoxy."[1] Unless the context makes it clear that we are speaking only of Protestant neo-orthodoxy or Catholic Vatican II efforts, we shall use the term "reformers" for both.

---

[1] Tracy, <u>Blessed Rage</u>, pp. 30, 38, n. 34 and especially p. 40, n. 54.

# Scripture Image and Implications

When COCU defined the Church as "truly reformed," the authors quickly declared "the Bible rightly portrays the Church as a people on pilgrimage (I Cor. 10:1-4; Heb. 11:29, 37-12:2)."[2] Affirming that "equal emphasis falls on both words," the authors then declared that "the Pilgrim Church . . . . lives in tension between the already and the not yet (Lk. 11:20; Matt. 6:10)."[3] Note the explicit reference to tension; this can be very creative, as we shall see below.

In an amazing convergence, the Constitution on the Church of Vatican II is full of the term "pilgrim people."[4] This image spread to many other documents of Vatican II.[5] (See also Decree on Missionary Activity cited in Introduction above, p. 4). One of the immediate consequences of this image is reform, or stripping down to the essentials. The model of a pilgrim Church means that something from the old home is preserved, but in its most essential and stripped down form. It will be transported to the new home, drastically changed but substantially the same.

The model of a pilgrim Church is a halfway model between the Body of Christ favored by catholics, and the People of God preferred by evangelicals. On pilgrimage, there are leaders, scouts, people with

---

[2] COCU, In Quest, 14a, p. 17 (underlining is italics in original); Consensus, 13a, p. 19.
[3] In Quest, 14a, p. 17; 18e, p. 18; Consensus, 13a, p. 19; 14, pp. 20-21.
[4] Constitution on the Church, #'s 8, 9, 48.
[5] Decree on Ecumenism, #'s 2-3, 6; Constitution on the Church in the Modern World, #45 and Revelation, #8.

defined responsibilities (the model "People" does not immediately imply this, while "Body" implies a certain rigidity of roles). Thus reformers are admirably suited to times of drastic change, as they seek to preserve the best of the past while jettisoning anything non-essential.

A closely related Scripture text centers on reconciliation. When American Presbyterians wrote their "Confession of 1967," neo-orthodoxy was at its height in the denomination. And they relied heavily on 2 Cor. 5:16-21, where Paul uses the term "reconciliation" five times, beginning with our reconciliation to God by Christ, and then extending to the ministry of reconciliation by the Church. Here the reformed attempt to hold together two opposing realities, sinful humanity and a gracious God.[6]

## Historical Overview

The great characteristic of the reformed, to reconcile tensions, is captured in the Epistle to Diognetus (c. 150), with its extraordinary series of contrasts:

> Christians love all men, but all men persecute them. . . .
> They live in poverty, but enrich many; they are totally
> destitute, but possess an abundance of everything. They
> suffer dishonor, but that is their glory. They are defamed,
> but vindicated.[7]

---

[6] See Edward A. Dowey, Jr., A Commentary on the Confession of 1967 and An Introduction to the Book of Confessions (Philadelphia, PA: Westminster, 1968), especially ch. 2, "Motif: Reconciliation," pp. 39-42.

[7] Used in Pope Paul VI, Liturgy of the Hours (New York, NY: Catholic Book Publishing Co., 1976) 2:841, probably echoing St. Paul's 2nd Letter to the Corinthians 6:8-10. Cited five times in the Catechism (Catholic). For a contemporary to Diognetus, see Liturgy of the Hours 3: 161-62.

The superior general of the Congregation of the Mission (Vincentians) used this text to conclude his New Testament reflections on paradox.[8]

The famous dictum of the Church Fathers, that Christians never say either/or but both/and, is a reflection of the reformed strand. Heresies result when one side forgets that Christ is <u>both</u> divine and human; God is infinite <u>and</u> we are free; God's grace and human works are <u>both</u> necessary, etc.[9]

"The Church Reformed, and Always in Need of Reformation" is another principle stressed from the Patristic period. The <u>Constitution on the Church</u> put it in blunt terms for Catholics: "at the same time holy and always in need of being purified."[10] Unfortunately, when the Protestant Reformation and the Catholic Counter-Reformation occurred in the 16th century, Protestants so stressed the need for reform, and Catholics so stressed the need for continuity, that both lost sight of the truth in the other's position. Certain Catholics still attempted, during the early Renaissance, to hold opposites together, as Cardinal Nicholas Cusa (1401-64) in his famous "Docta Ignorantia" (learned ignorance).[11] But they were few and far between.

---

[8] Robert P. Maloney, C.M., "An Upside-Down Sign: The Church of Paradox," <u>America</u>, Nov. 22, 1997, pp. 6-11

[9] . John Macquarrie finds this especially true in Karl Rahner, <u>Principles of Christian Theology</u> (NY: Scribners, 1977), 98, 2nd ed., p. vii.

[10] <u>Constitution on the Church</u>, #8 (see especially n. 25, p. 23, Abbott); <u>Decree on Ecumenism</u>, #6; <u>Catechism</u> (Catholic), #827.

[11] J. Koch, "Nicholas of Cusa," <u>New Catholic Encyclopedia</u> (Washington, D.C.: Catholic University of America, 1967): 10:449-52.

The 400 years from about 1550 to 1950 found the word "reform" practically dropping out of Catholic vocabulary, and being monopolized by the Protestant Churches coming directly from the 16th century Reformation. Pope St. Pius X did restore Communion as an integral part of Mass,[12] and Pius XII did return the Easter Triduum to its rightful time.[13] But these reforms were practical, lacking a comprehensive doctrinal framework.

With the publication by Karl Barth of <u>Commentary on the Epistle to the Romans</u> (1918), things began to slowly change. Historical consciousness began to emerge in practically all corners of Christianity. And historical consciousness meant that both Catholics and Protestants tried to preserve the best of the past while addressing sympathetically the needs of the present.

Welch calls Barth's commentary "a book of violent protest against the fundamental premises of 'liberal' theology."[14] H. Richard Niebuhr criticized the liberalism of the 1920's in a classic sentence: "A God without wrath brought men without sin into a kingdom without judgment through the ministrations of a Christ without a cross."[15] (He might have added, "through Scripture without relevance.") Niebuhr thus tells us that neo-orthodoxy insisted <u>on joining</u> God's love and God's

---

[12] Pius X, <u>Sacra Tridentina</u>, in <u>Christian Faith</u>, 1209/1-4.
[13] Pius XII, March 15, 1956, Congregation of Rites.
[14] Claude Welch and John Dillenberger, <u>Protestant Christianity</u> (New York, NY: Scribner's, 1954), p. 255.
[15] H. Richard Niebuhr, <u>The Kingdom of God in America</u> (Chicago, IL: University of Chicago Press, 1937), p. 193.

wrath; humanity's goodness and humanity's sinfulness; the Church's mercy and the Church's judgment; the resurrection and the cross. And Biblical theology developed and was valued as perhaps never before.

Led by the Swiss-born Barth, and joined by the German-born Paul Tillich, neo-orthodox theologians respected the complaints of liberal theologians that the Bible had to be interpreted for modern people. Some parts, like the story of creation in Genesis, could not be taken literally. But unlike the liberals, the neo-orthodox, by emphasizing God's revelation to humanity, gave "a far more important place to the Bible than was characteristic of liberalism and involves at least a partial return to the classical Protestant norm of sola Sciptura" (Scripture alone).[16]

Catholics, who at this same time were going through the difficulty of reconciling the Bible's worldview with modern science, quickly noted the sturdier place of the Bible in neo-orthodoxy. The Scottish Presbyterian William Barclay's Scripture work became the Catholic Bishop Fulton Sheen's favorite daily mediation long before Vatican II brought Catholic and Protestant emphasis on the Bible closer together.[17]

The classic story of the convergence of Protestant neo-orthodox and Catholic reformers is related by R.M. Brown. The young Catholic theologian Hans Kung did his doctoral thesis (1964) comparing justification in Karl Barth and the Council of Trent. Barth stated Kung interpreted him correctly (therefore, he must have misinterpreted Trent).

---

[16] Welch, Protestant Christianity, p. 275.
[17] Fulton J. Sheen, Treasure in Clay (Image, 1982), p. 79.

Catholic reviewers stated Kung interpreted Trent correctly (therefore, he must have misinterpreted Barth). "Kung's amazing discovery is that what Karl Barth says about justification is what the Tridentine fathers were really trying to say, when understood in their historical and polemical context."[18]

Sometimes described as the grandfather of Vatican II, Cardinal John Henry Newman (1801-90) coined the phrase which helped develop the historical consciousness of both Protestants and Catholics. "To live here below is to change, and to be perfect is to change often."[19]

I shall never forget being in St. Peter's Square on that memorable day when the Second Vatican Council opened, October 11, 1962. My classmates and I had been studying in Latin since October 1958, and we clearly understood the shocking implications of what Pope John XXIII (1881-1963) said that day. First he attacked some of his collaborators in the Vatican, calling them "prophets of gloom," and describing how he had to listen "much to our regret, to voices of persons who, though burning with zeal, are not endowed with too much sense of discretion or measure."[20] For a pope to publicly attack those who worked with him was unheard of.

But he didn't stop there. He introduced, or re-introduced, a principle which had been absent from Catholic discourse for 400 years.

---

[18] R.M Brown,. Ecumenical Revolution, p. 100.
[19] John Henry Newman, An Essay on the Development of Christian Doctrine, ch. 1, sec. 1, p. 24.
[20] Abbott, "Pope John's Opening Speech," Documents of Vatican II, p. 712.

"The substance of the ancient doctrine of the deposit of faith is one thing, and the way in which it is presented is another."[21]

Two theologians had prepared the way for Pope John's work, often at great personal suffering: the Jesuit Karl Rahner (1904-84) and the Dominican Yves M.J. Congar (1904-95). Their achievements are immense. The best place to begin to explore them is the appreciation of each written in America at their deaths.[22]

J.H. Nichols, in his capacity at the first session of Vatican II as an observer for the World Alliance of Presbyterian and Reformed Churches, noted quickly the growing historical consciousness promoted by the council. He pointed out the convergence between the "Confession of 1967" (American Presbyterians) and the documents of Vatican II: they both represented "high historical consciousness."[23]

A professor at United Presbyterian Pittsburgh Theological Seminary wrote that the process of debating the Confession made his denomination "more catholic, evangelical and reformed than ever before."[24] We now have a convergence of COCU terms, Presbyterian heritage, and Catholic Vatican II updating.

---

[21] Ibid, p. 715.

[22] For Rahner, see America, June 16, 1984, pp. 452-59 (notice in April 14, pp. 270-71); for Congar, see July 15, 1995, pp. 6-7; Aug. 12, pp. 23-25; Sept. 30, p. 30.

[23] James Hastings Nichols, "Ecumenical Aspects of Confession of 1967," Ecumenist 6 (1967, 1):107.

[24] John Gerstner, "New Light on the Confession of 1967," Christianity Today, Dec. 9, 1966, p. 246.

# Apologies and Reparation

The Catholic Church joined the ecumenical movement officially with Vatican II's Decree on Ecumenism. In it, for the first time in 400 years, the Catholic Church admitted that the blame for divisions within Christianity lay on "both sides."[25] And explicitly, "for sins against unity. . . . we beg pardon of God and of our separated brethren, just as we forgive them that trespass against us."[26] Now catholics in all Churches were challenged to admit mistakes; a convergence of apologies began.

In 1978, on the 15th anniversary of the <u>Constitution on Liturgy</u>, the U.S. Bishops Committee on Liturgy admitted publicly that healing was needed after the firestorm of changes in worship initiated by Vatican II.

> We realize that in the renewal process some—clergy and laity alike—have been hurt. There are those who were hurt simply by the phenomenon of change, the removal of the familiar, and the uncertainty of the untried and untested Still others were hurt by poor instruction, left ill-prepared for what was introduced, or misguided by the conduct of enthusiasts. Moreover, we cannot forget those who were hurt in the very process of implementing the reform—greeted with ridicule, hostility, at times refusal.
> Confident of the soundness of the renewal, as designed by the providentially inspired guidance of the Church, we all must strive to overcome any divisiveness or rancor. Let time, humility, and love work in the hearts of all to heal the wounds so that we may remain united in belief and practice (See: I Cor 1:11).[27]

I find the statement noteworthy for two reasons. First, it probably

---

[25] Abbott, <u>Decree on Ecumenism</u>, #3; see also #6, (pp. 345, 350).

[26] Ibid, #7, (citing I Jo 1:10), p. 351.

[27] U.S. Bishops Committee on Liturgy, "A Commemorative Statement," <u>Bishops Committee on the Liturgy</u> Newsletter, Dec. 1978, p. 143. For the 20th anniversary statement, see <u>Newsletter</u>, Dec. 1983, p. 46.

shocked American Catholics by its blunt admission of failures. Secondly, most Christians in our times have endured similar experiences with changes in worship.

In 1991, the Missionary Oblates in Canada attempted to apologize to the native peoples. Unfortunately, the leadership of the Oblates did not attempt to obtain a consensus from our own members beforehand, and there was a significant backlash.[28]

Pope John Paul II insisted on apologizing. Some 94 times, in 21 different areas, beginning very early in his administration, he has set the example for Catholics.[29] However, in 1994, he aroused opposition from close advisors when he published his plan for the 2000 millennium. John Thavis, writing in the Catholic News Service, noted that "the cardinals' reaction was lukewarm; to many, this was the proverbial can of worms."[30]

In 1995, Southern Baptists attracted much attention by wrestling with the heritage of slavery, "this dirty linen in the closet."[31]

At the Conference on World Mission and Evangelism held by the World Council of Churches in Salvador, Bahia, Brazil, Nov. 2-Dec. 3, 1996, an apology was made which caught the attention of many, many people. "During a ceremony of common confession of sins, it was not

---

[28] Canadian Oblates, "An Apology to Native Peoples," Origins 21 (August, 15, 1991, #11): 183-84, with response in Kerygma 25 (1991, #57): 141-58 (Now Mission)

[29] The 94 times are presented by Luigi Accattoli, When A Pope Asks Forgiveness (Canfield, OH: Alba House, 1998).

[30] John Thavis, "A 'mea culpa' from Rome," Catholic Sun (Syracuse, NY), Dec. 1-7, 1994, p. P15, quoting more fully Cardinal Clancy of Australia and Cardinal Meisner of Germany.

[31] Adelle M. Banks, Religion News Service, Washington Post, June 10, 1995, p. H11.

only the leading role played by the colonialists in the slavery that was remembered, but also the African participation and responsibility in it."[32] Forgiveness is most effective when both sides admit at least some responsibility.

All during this time, Catholics were wrestling with past conduct towards Jews. In 1998, the Vatican issued <u>We Remember: A Reflection on the Shoah</u>. Cardinal Edward Cassidy, who signed the document, was quoted as explaining that the church, as a human institution (in distinction as the Body of Christ on earth) can sin, and needs to constantly repent.[33]

Archbishop Alex Burnet of Seattle, WA, in the Sixth Paul Wattson Lecture (St. Mary's University, Halifax, Nova Scotia), related how during the Week of Prayer for Christian Unity in Rome, Jan. 18, 2000, the pope invited other church leaders to join him in opening the Holy Door at St Paul's Basilica. Flanked by Archbishop George Carey (Anglican) and the representative of the Ecumenical Patriarch of Constantinople, he pushed on the door, and it would not open. "It was only when he was joined in the effort . . . that the massive door yielded to the joint touch of all three ecumenical leaders."[34]

On the First Sunday of Lent, March 12, 2000, the pope offered the

---

[32] Jacques Matthey, "Salvador Among the World Mission Conferences of This Century," <u>International Review of Mission</u> 86 (1997, #'s 340-41, Jan./April): 22.

[33] Eugene J. Fisher, "Catholics and Jews Confront The Holocaust and Each Other," <u>America</u>, Sept. 11, 1999, p. 12.

[34] Most Rev. Alex J. Brunett, "Harvesting the Past, Planning for the Future: Our Pilgrimage Together," <u>Ecumenical Trends</u> 30 (Feb. 2001, #2): 1/17. We will use the 11 page speech again: highly recommended.

much awaited apology, "an act virtually unprecedented in the history of the Catholic magisterium" (teaching office).[35] The Jesuit theologian Francis Sullivan offered the most accessible explanation of this act.[36] In words reminiscent of the Presbyterian Confession of 1967's emphasis on reconciliation (although not actually using the word), he stated: The Church "is also in a certain sense sinner, in really taking upon herself the sin of those whom she has generated in Baptism. This is analogous to the way Christ Jesus took on the sin of the World."[37]

The pope's cry "We forgive and we ask forgiveness," noted America, "was echoed by local churches in the United States and elsewhere and generally welcomed by non-Catholics around the world."[38] The response of the United Methodists came quickly.[39] But perhaps the most moving came only four days later, in the Catholic-Pentecostal meeting mentioned in ch. 2, above. On March 16, Father McDonnell "in a private capacity," but none the less very effectively, sought "forgiveness" for the sins that Catholics had committed against Pentecostals. On March 18, at the close of the meeting, Professor Frank Macchia (Pentecostal) offered "a corresponding request for forgiveness."[40]

---

[35] Elizabeth H. Mellen, "Introducing this issue," Ecumenical Trends 29 (Nov. 2000, #10): 1/145.

[36] Francis A. Sullivan, S.J., "The Papal Apology," America, April 8, 2000, pp. 17-19, 22.

[37] Sullivan, quoting the International Theological Commission, Memory and Reconciliation: The Church and the Faults of the Past, America, p. 18. He "would have preferred" the Vatican II notion of the church as the "pilgrim people of God" (p. 22).

[38] Unsigned "News," America, March 25, 2000, giving many examples, pp. 4-5.

[39] National Catholic Register, April 2-8, 2000, p. 1; America, May 27, 2000, p. 5.

[40] The entire issue of Ecumenical Trends 29 (Nov. 2000, #10) is devoted to the meeting, which treated Proselytism and Common Witness. McDonnell's apology is on pp. 15/159-16/160; Robeck's, 16/160.

During the pope's visit to Greece in 2001, he again asked forgiveness, this time from the Orthodox, who had indicated very clearly that his visit was unwelcome.[41]

On October 24, 2001, the pope "apologized for any actions taken by Catholics that offended China or gave an impression of disrespect for its culture."[42] Hopefully, these apologies will aid the convergence of not only Catholics and Orthodox, but all Christians, for mission.

On June 13, 2002, the president of the U.S. Conference of Catholic Biships "apologized profusely to victims of sexual abuse by priests, to their families, to religious, deacons and laity, and to 'our faithful priests'."[43]

My own experience indicates that the apology must be carefully prepared. During the 75th anniversary of St. Rose of Lima Parish, Buffalo, NY, (2000) various groups within the parish were asked to prepare an apology about the way certain personalities or issues hindered the mission of the parish. During the First Friday evening Benediction, most of the parish leaders publicly expressed their regrets. Attendance by parishioners was, however, disappointing.[44]

---

[41] See David Carlson's very moving description, "Bearing One Another's Burdens," Ecumenical Trends 31 (June, 2002, #6) 12/92-14/94.

[42] America, Nov. 5, 2001, p. 5.

[43] "New," America, July 1-8, 2002, p. 6. For a significant analysis of this event invoking Vatican II's pilgrim model, see Christopher Ruddy, "The American Church's Sexual Abuse Crisis," America, June 3-10, 2002, pp. 7-11.

[44] Harry Winter, O.M.I., editor, St. Rose's 75th Memory Booklet, p. 10.

# A Spirituality of Tensions

When Father Henri Nouwen authored The Wounded Healer, he practically summarized a favorite theme of reformers. Both sides of the tension must be maintained.[45] Perhaps the most challenging tension is that of Word and Sacrament. Evangelicals tended to stress the preaching part of the Sunday service, built around extensive use of Scripture. Catholics tended to stress the sacramental part, especially the Lord's Supper, and neglect the Scripture. Father Norm Bonneau, in his masterful explanation of the Sunday three-year lectionary now shared by many Christian Churches, has concluded: "Now Catholics see that the Word provides the 'why' of sacrament and Reformed Churches recognize that the Word must be 'enfleshed' in Sacrament."[46] Reformers among the Catholics at Vatican II, and especially in the United Presbyterian Church USA, brought this about, and it is a most creative tension.[47]

The late Scripture Scholar Father Raymond Brown summed up a fundamental tension between clergy sharing in "ordinary life and problems," and clergy being dedicated to God, somewhat separated. He ties this into the Biblical problem mentioned above of integrating the priesthood of the Old Testament into the presbyterate of the New.[48]

---

[45] Henri Nouwen, The Wounded Healer (Garden City, NY: Image Books, 1972).

[46] Norm Bonneau, O.M.I., The Sunday Lectionary (Collegeville, MN: Liturgical Press, 1998), p. 54.

[47] Harry E. Winter, O.M.I., "Presbyterians Pioneer the Vatican II Sunday Lectionary," Journal of Ecumenical Studies, 38 (Spring-Summer, 2001, #2-3): 148-50.

[48] Raymond Brown, S.S., Responses to 101 Questions on the Bible (Mahwah, NJ: Paulist. 1990), p. 126 (Question 96).

Karl Rahner was a master at reconciling tension. Perhaps his best explanation of the way that faith and doubt coexist is his question: "If there is necessarily a Catholic simul iustus et peccator [both just and sinful], why is there not necessarily a Catholic, Christian simul fidelis et infidelis [both faithful and unfaithful]?"[49]

Martin Marty's works on religion and politics carry on the Reformation challenge to the state. The Public Religion Program, sponsored by the Pew Trust, has given him a valuable forum: two volumes have already appeared, trying to balance the role of religion, and still respect those who are indifferent or antagonistic to religion.[50]

After the events of September 11, 2001, more has been written about the tension between waging peace and preparing for war.[51] William Bole, an associate fellow of the Woodstock Theological Center at Georgetown University, Washington, DC, cited Hanna Arendt:

> Forgiveness is compatible with justice, never with vengeance. As Hanna Arendt said, human beings cannot forgive what they cannot punish.[52]

Liberals tend to view history as a progress ever upward, especially since the Enlightenment. Fundamentalists tent to view history as ever worsening. Reformed indicate that both are happening. Father Louis

---

[49] Karl Rahner, S.J., <u>Servants of the Lord</u> (New York, NY: Herder, 1968), p. 49. The entire book is classic Rahnerian concrete spirituality.

[50] Martin E Marty. with Jonathan Moore, <u>Politics, Religion and the Common Good</u> (Jossey-Bass, Inc., 2000), reviewed by John A. Coleman, S.J., <u>America</u>, July 15-22, 2000, pp. 24-25; <u>Education, Religion and the Common Good</u> (Jossey-Bass, 2000), Coleman, <u>America</u>, Dec. 16, 2000, pp. 14-15.

[51] See for example the widely circulated questions and answers from the (Catholic) <u>Catechism</u>, #'s 2302-2317, used in the newsletter for October, 2001 of WLOF Catholic Radio, Buffalo, NY, p.. 3.

[52] William Bole, "Forgive—and Punish," <u>Catholic Northwest Progress</u>, Oct. 18, 2001, p. 9.

Hertling, a Jesuit historian, used the following illustration in 1962: the line is continually up, but there are times when we fall far below the upward thrust.[53]

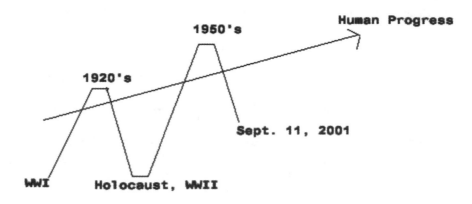

## Reformed and the Death Penalty

Because of their insistence on original sin, and its pervasiveness even after baptism, reformed theologians agree with C.S. Lewis' endorsement of capital punishment. It is "perfectly right for a Christian judge to sentence a man to death or a Christian soldier to kill an enemy."[54] And Reinhold Niebuhr, in his classic Moral Man and Immoral Society stated clearly that his opponents were "wrong in their assumption that violence is intrinsically immoral. Nothing is intrinsically immoral except ill-will and nothing is intrinsically good except

---

[53] Louis Hertling, S.J., Early Church History Course, Autumn, 1962, Gregorian University, Rome, Italy. Hertling drew the general illustration on the backboard; I have used my own examples.
[54] C.S. Lewis, Mere Christianity (NY: Macmillan, 1960), rev. ed., p. 106.

goodwill."[55]

Note that the reformed try boldly to hold together the positions of liberals who reject the death penalty because of the execution of innocent people, with the position of the evangelicals, that no forgiveness is possible without justice. Niebuhr stated frankly, in a broader context of reconciling the inner life of the individual with the same individual's social obligations, that it is "a constant and seemingly irreconcilable conflict."[56]

## Reformation of Christology and Mariology

Perhaps the most stunning and unobserved reform of doctrine are the two agreements with several pre-Orthodox Eastern Churches. At the third ecumenical council (Ephesus, 431), Nestorius was condemned for his views that Mary should not be called the Mother of God (Theotokos) The Assyrian Church split with the united Eastern and Western church over this issue. In 1994, Pope John Paul II and the Assyrian Patriarch Mar Dinkha IV signed a declaration affirming their Christological unity which "respects Assyrian sensibilities by not insisting on the Mariological title Theotokos as absolutely essential."[57]

At the fourth ecumenical council (Chalcedon, 451), Eastern and Western Churches agreed on Jesus being one person in two natures

---

[55] Reinhold Niebuhr, Moral Man and Immoral Society (NY: Schribner, 1932, with 1960 preface), p. 170 (see 171-75).
[56] Ibid, p. 251.
[57] Jeff Gros, et al., Introduction to Ecumenism, p. 157.

(human and divine). Armenian, Coptic, Ethiopian, Syrian, Malankara Syrian, and Eritrean (Oriental Orthodox Churches) left over this issue, both with Eastern (Greek) Orthodoxy, and the Western (Latin) Church. Ecumenical dialogue between Rome and these churches now concludes that they mean the same when they speak of Christ's personality, divinity and humanity; full union would not require their allegiance to the formula of Chalcedon.[58]

For centuries, the definitions of these two councils were considered irreformable. Now Rome and the Oriental Orthodox Churches have moderated positions in a remarkable way. Ronald Roberson concludes his examination of the situation:

> A careful reading of the statements issued over the past 30 years indicates that the ancient Christological dispute between the Oriental Orthodox churches and the Catholic Church has been substantially resolved. . . . their faith in the mystery of Christ which transcends all formulations is, in fact, the same.[59]

We have seen how the issue of justification, which bedeviled Lutheran and Roman Catholic relations, has been largely solved (above, p. 64). Now the decisions of ancient ecumenical councils have, in a sense, been put to one side. Can the disputes between Catholics and Protestants over papacy, Eucharistic presence, etc. be put to the side in the same way?

---

[58] Ibid, pp. 157-63.
[59] Ronald Roberson, C.S.P., The Eastern Christian Churches, p. 246.

## The Reformed Position in Decline, and Rebirth?

One of the weaknesses of the reformed position was its tendency to use academic and technical language. In the debate among Presbyterians over the Confession of 1967, the theologians used the expression "normative" for Scripture, reserving "authoritative" only for Christ. But many people objected, saying that "normative" was too weak a word in ordinary language to convey what the Presbyterian Church wished to state. So the use of "authoritative" was accepted as applying to Scripture.[60]

COCU had noted very early that the reformed element differed from the catholic and evangelical element.[61] More of a corrective than a full-fledged strand, the reformed were found in most surveys as fewer than other categories. Carl F.H. Henry, for example, noted:

> In 1957 a professional sampling of the theological convictions of American clergy showed that 14 per cent identified themselves as liberal, 12 per cent as neo-orthodox, and 75 per cent as either conservative or fundamentalist.[62]

In 1972, only seven years after Vatican II ended, editors Alois Muller and Norbert Greinacher were writing in Concilium:

> Church reform, which was experienced in the period of the Council as an overdue and happy change, has now become a weary business when the powers who oppose it appear without any mask, and the forces of reform have

---

[60] See Christianity Today 18 June, 1965, pp. 1004-05, and Quebedeaux's comment, The Young Evangelicals, p. 38.

[61] Consultation on Church Union, Principles (Cincinnati: Forward Movement Publications, 1966), p. 62.

[62] Carl F.H. Henry, "Evangelicals and Ecumenism," Christianity Today, May 27, 1966, p. 11.

largely lost their joy and courage.[63]

The very articulate voice of neo-orthodoxy, the bi-weekly journal Christianity and Crisis, folded in April, 1993. Begun with eight pages during the dark days of World War II (the first issue was on Feb. 10, 1941), it had grown to about 25 pages an issue. Reinhold Niebuhr was chair of the editorial board; its pages show very well the concerns and voices of the reformed.[64]

A Presbyterian leader in the effort to use a common lectionary has described the tension in worship for his Church (and all Churches): "a constant dialectic between constitution and congregation, between form and freedom, between structure and spontaneity."[65] Preserving tensions, however, is energy-consuming and extremely difficult. The lessening of reformed impact may be best shown in the Presbyterian Church, which probably had the highest percentage of reformed. Since the mid-1960's to 1993, the Presbyterian Church USA lost about one-third of its membership, dropping to 2.8 million.[66]

Prophetic leadership is expensive. Stated Clerk Eugene Carson Blake was a foremost figure in integration; Christian Education leader

---

[63] Alois Muller and Norbert Greinacher, "Editorial," Ongoing Reform of the Church (NY: Herder, 1972), Concilium, #73, p. 8.

[64] Reinhold Niebuhr, "The Christian Faith and the World Crisis," Christianity and Crisis, Feb. 10, 1941 (vol. 1, #1): 4-6. The last issue was April 12, 1993, vol. 53, #4); it is full of articles (37 pp.) which end its career with a trumpet blast, not a whimper.

[65] Horace Allen, Reformed Liturgy & Music 27 (Winter, 1993, #1): 14, resorting to Calvin's favorite text (I Cor. 14:39-40) "all things should be done decently and in order."

[66] Religious News Service, June 12, 1993; Dean Hoge, Benton Johnson and Don Luidens did a thorough study on why people join and leave Presbyterianism: Vanishing Boundaries (Louisville, KY: Westminster John Knox Press, 1993.

Harold Davis (Cumberland Presbyterian Church, working closely with PCUSA) took a prominent role in Martin Luther King's effort to integrate sanitation workers in Memphis.[67] In the early 1970's, the United Presbyterian Council of Church and Race made $10,000.00 available to Communist sympathizer Angela Davis' defense fund; "record numbers" left.[68]

The success of some issues they espoused, and the over-extension into other issues, may explain partially why the reformed position has grown less prominent. However, on September 11, 2001, the relative peacefulness of the 1980's and 1990's came to a shattering end. As we shall see in ch. 5, the liberalism of the Clinton years was reversed not only by George Bush's razor thin 2000 election, but especially by the War Against Terrorism. The reformed came to prominence partly because of the Great Depression and World War II. The reformed now have a new relevance.

With the waning of the tragedy of the concentration camps and World War II, there was certainly less visibility of the evil side of human nature which had so impressed Barth. But one thing we may be sure of: when tragedies do occur on a large scale, such as the Sept. 11 event, the need to balance justice and mercy does appear again.

---

[67] Harry Winter, O.M.I., "Presbyterians Pioneer the Vatican II Lectionary," Journal of Ecumenical Studies, 38:141.

[68] Betty Medsger, Washington Post, June 19, 1971, B6. Presbyterian Life, the denominational magazine peaked at 1,158,058 in 1962; by 1972, it had declined to 642,182.

Gary Larson's cartoon is all too familiar to the reformed.[69]  It shows a cowboy, full of arrows like a pincushion, riding from the far side of the cartoon, where he has been negotiating with the Indians.  As he approaches the near side, where his buddies are gathered, one buddy says to the other:  "Now stay calm. . . Let's hear what they said to Bill."

Reformers feel very strongly the pain of being caught between two sides.  Yet, they would be uncomfortable on either side; they, by inclination and conviction, are mediators, bridges, and the bonding element in Christianity, as painful as that is.

Most pastors during the 1970's and 1980's awoke one morning to discover that every family in the parish was afflicted by at least one of three major problems:  terminal illness such as cancer; divorce, or substance abuse (alcohol and drugs).  This was certainly not the case in the 1950's.  I believe that parish staff people who continually deal with such problems are very likely to be either reformed, or sympathetic to the reformed way.[70]

## Paradox, Tensions and Pilgrimage as the Millennium Began

The continual interest in G.K. Chesterton probably is due at least in part to reformed Christians' love of paradox.  A 1998 biography was

---

[69] Gary Larson, The Far Side, (Fairway, KS:  Andrews and McMeel, Inc., 1984), n.p., 3rd cartoon..
[70] My discovery of this happened in the early 1980's, when I was a pastor in Appalachia, and was described as it affected my next parish: "Multicultural Parishes," America, Jan. 27, 1996, p. 10.

reviewed with the description "with typical Chestertonian paradox."[71]

Rolheiser, in a 1999 column, explicitly links paradox with holding

two truths in tension. (Another image, that of bridges, means that

reformed Christians will bear heavy burdens of holding two sides

together). Rolheiser concluded his column:

> Great truth is found in paradox and those who try to find
> it will also find themselves having to sweat blood in the
> garden, not knowing on any given day which pole to honor,
> but knowing always that fidelity lies in respecting both sides
> in the paradox.[72]

Cardinal Walter Kasper, president of the Pontifical council for

Promoting Christian Unity, gently but firmly disagreed with the emphasis

of Cardinal Joseph Ratzinger on the relationship of the universal church,

and particular (local) churches. Kasper's approach can be called

reformed, as he explicitly seeks to hold in creative tension both the

universal church, and the local church.[73]

A Native American archbishop, Charles Chaput commented on

Kasper's article with a tension of his own, between change and stability,

especially in the liturgy. He drew deeply from Eastern theology, yet

wondered if that would work in the U.S.A.[74]

Rolheiser, in a 2001 column, noted that tensions tend to be

---

[71] Joseph J. Feeney, S.J., reviewing Joseph Pearce, Wisdom and Innocence: A Life of G. K. Chesterton (Ignatius Press, 1998), America, April 4, 1998, p. 32.

[72] Ronald Rolheiser, "Truth is Found in Paradox," Catholic Northwest Progress, Jan. 14, 1999, p. 14.

[73] Walter Kasper, "On the Church," America, April 23-30, 2001, pp. 8-14; see above ch. 1, sect. 2, n. 13.

[74] Charles J. Chaput, "Reflections on Walter Kasper's 'On the Church'," America, July 30-Aug. 6, 2001, pp. 18-19.

"imperialistic," each pole wanting all of us.[75]  A November column movingly describes the urgent need to balance the ordinary and extraordinary in our existence.[76]

The French Catholic missionary in India, Lucien Legrand, has a telling comparison in his much praised Unity and Plurality:  Mission in the Bible.

> Paul VI unintentionally aroused a hostile reaction when he declared, in Bombay, that his journey to India was a "missionary" journey.  Doubtless he meant that he had come not as a statesman, but as a priest.  Still the very word was enough to raise hackles.  John Paul II styled his own trip a "pilgrimage."  There was more than a more judicious, more diplomatic choice of words here.  The change in vocabulary reflected a raised consciousness of mission.  Here was a new awareness of a mission in the image of Jesus' own mission: a humble, serving mission, which consisted not only in speaking, but in listening, as well.[77]

By May, 2001, when the pope traveled to Greece, Syria and Malta, John Thavis was able to write "he was traveling not as a religious tourist and not as a political negotiator, but as a pilgrim convinced that God has spoken to humanity in all these places—and continues to speak to the men and women of today."[78]

David Bosch gives a very balanced description of the way Christianity affects all cultures, and is affected by them.[79]  The reformed Christian senses very strongly that "Christianity can never renounce its

---

[75] Ronald Rolheiser, O.M.I., "The Tension Between Theology and Piety," The Catholic Northwest Progress, Feb. 15, 2001, p. 14.

[76] Ibid,  "In Praise of the Ordinary," Nov. 1, 2001, p. 15.

[77] Lucian Legrand, Unity and Plurality (Maryknoll, NY:  Orbis, 1990), p. xiv.

[78] John Thavis, CNS, "Pope Travels to Revive the Roots of Faith," Catholic Northwest Progress, May 10, 2001, p. 2.

[79] David Bosch, Transforming Mission, pp. 381-89 (also 291-98).

claim to judge all cultures."[80] Yet at the same time the reformed evangelizer knows that our message is always in need of aggiornamento, renewal and reform.

We now turn to the two models which differ most widely on reforming the Christian message.

---

[80] Harry E. Winter, O.M.I., "Ecumenical Strategy for Evangelization," <u>Mission in Dialogue</u>, p. 219.

CHAPTER FOUR: FUNDAMENTALIST CHRISTIANITY

## Overview

On Sept. 11, 2001, a group of Islamic fundamentalists attacked the United States of America, and through this attack, Western civilization. Moderate Islam rejected this group.

However, the United States itself responded with a fundamentalist instinct: it emphasized basic or fundamental values—family, faith, patriotism. As Christians reject extreme forms of fundamentalism within Christianity, we need to remember that the fundamentalist instinct is a survival instinct shared by all religions and cultures. As such, it has appeared from the earliest days of Christianity, and will continue to appear, especially when Christianity is severely threatened.

Any group will tilt towards fundamentalism when it is in danger. Terms such as fortress mentality, siege mentality, or circling the wagons describe what happens to the entire organization when it is faced with a real threat. We will not be using fundamentalism in this sense unless it is explicitly noted.

The fundamentalism we are discussing, within both Catholicism and Protestantism, concerns groups that cannot come out of the fortress when the danger has passed, which see the threat as the only factor in their existence. Since the 1980's, and especially since Sept. 11, 2001, this strand has been growing stronger. Catholic author Father Robert J.

Fox put it this way: "Fundamentalism is considered one of the greatest dangers today to mainline Protestantism and Roman Catholicism." [1]

## A Note Regarding Fundamentalism, Conservatism and Liberalism

All fundamentalists are conservative, but not all conservatives are fundamentalists. The political satirist Andy Rooney listed the opposing traits of conservatives and liberals in his column of January 31, 2001. Two which concern us most directly:

> Conservatives are more religious than liberals—although there is no evidence that they're nicer people because of it. . . . Conservatives oppose abortion and liberal Democrats do not. No one knows why this is a liberal/conservative issue.[2]

Large numbers of catholics and evangelical/charismatics are conservative. Many reformed are sympathetic to conservatism, if not outright participants. Stressing the past, continuity, and tradition shows a conservative side. But as Rooney noted: "not all liberals are liberal about everything and not all conservatives are conservative about everything."[3]

Conservatives tend to defend the status quo, especially in religion. Liberals tend to question, update, and seek relevancy. Fundamentalists are the most rigid of conservatives, and are almost obsessed with preserving their basic values. A true fundamentalist embraces <u>all</u>

---

[1] Robert J. Fox, Protestant Fundamentalism & the Born-Again-Catholic (Alexandria, SD: Fatima Family Apostolate, 1990), p. 1.
[2] Andy Rooney, "On Liberals and Conservatives," Buffalo News, Jan. 31, 2001, p. B-5. See also Sept 20, 2000, p. B-9.
[3] Ibid, Jan. 31, 2001, p. B-5.

conservative traits, and does so rigidly. Evangelicals, on the other hand, are more concerned with the adult conversion experience, and its implications. Fundamentalists tend to submerge the adult conversion experience. Martin Marty has observed: "Evangelicalism and fundamentalism are by no means the same thing."[4]

Popular literature cites this description: A conservative is a liberal who has been mugged; a liberal is a conservative whose food stamps have run out.[5] Or in a quote attributed to Benjamin Disraeli: A man who is not a Liberal at sixteen has no heart; a man who is not a Conservative at sixty has no head.[6]

Jesuit theologian Patrick Arnold, in a very accessible analysis of fundamentalism, describes its being obsessed by the "myth of the Golden Age." He presents Shiite revolutionaries, ultra orthodox Israelis, Protestant "evangelicals" and Catholic fundamentalists, each with their own Golden Age.[7] Of course, the most recognizable of the Catholic groups is Archbishop Lefebvre's, whose Golden Age is the period following the Council of Trent, with the Tridentine Mass. Arnold notes, however, that, for most Catholic fundamentalists, the more fatal attraction is toward authority. (For Protestants, it is the Bible). "Liberal Catholicism is most objectionable precisely in its emphasis on personal

---

[4] Martin E. Marty, The Public Church: Mainline-Evangelical-Catholic (NY, NY; Crossroad, 1981), p. 12.
[5] See George W. Hunt, S.J., "Of Many Things," America, March 1986, p. 148.
[6] Hunt, ibid.
[7] Patrick M. Arnold, S.J., "The Rise of Catholic Fundamentalism," America, April 11, 1987, pp. 300-01.

responsibility and conscience and its provisions for greater participation in ecclesial decision-making by the laity." Of course, authority by Rome is only good when it agrees with the Catholic fundamentalist: teaching on economic, racial and social responsibility may be rejected.[8]

Liberalism perceives itself to be ahead of the mainstream, almost leading it into the future. Conservatism holds the mainstream together. Fundamentalism wants to stop the stream, and if fundamentalism is severely threatened, it will attempt to destroy the stream.

The Catholic lay apologist Karl Keating warns us that millions of evangelicals (and conservatives?), "who shun the label [of fundamentalism] are theologically fundamentalists."[9] For most people, the appeal to basics runs very, very deep, and the return to basics appears and re-appears constantly.

The Dominican theologian Thomas O'Meara stresses the conservative side of religion. "Religion and church are essentially conservative. People draw close to religion and its forms because they need a power and truth beyond them."[10] (O'Meara also demands a liberal side to religion, as we shall see in ch. 5).

Fundamentalists are cantankerous evangelicals. The fundamentalist authority George Marsden puts it this way: "A

---

[8] Ibid, pp. 301.
[9] Karl Keating, Catholicism and Fundamentalism (San Francisco, CA: Ignatius Press, 1988), p. 11.
[10] Thomas F. O'Meara, O.P., Fundamentalism: A Catholic Perspective (Mahwah, NJ: Paulist, 1990), p. 78 (see also 22, 51).

fundamentalist is an evangelical who is angry about something. . . . a religious conservative" who is "willing to stand and to fight."[11]

## Scripture Model and Implications

Fundamentalism uses Scripture images of the Church which are solid, permanent and stable.  Vatican II's Constitution on the Church began with an emphasis on the Church militant, a very stable image, and only later evolved into a document balancing stable images (house, temple, Holy City, New Jerusalem:  #6) with pilgrim (#8).[12]  Certainly the Catholic Church entered the Vatican II period with a strong sympathy towards fundamentalism:  the initial drafts of documents reflect this.[13]

I am convinced that an examination of hymns dear to fundamentalists would show this appeal of Scripture images which are unchanging and solid.  The appeal of the Church as the Holy City, the New Jerusalem (Rev. 21, used in #6 of C. on Church) reflects an image which does not change.  A fortified city in Biblical times couldn't change easily, or it lost its strong protection.[14]

Luther's famous hymn "A Mighty Fortress Is Our God," reflects the fundamentalist sympathy of the most conservative of all the 16th century Reformers:  Christ's Church is a fortress, of safety and security for all

---

[11] George M. Marsden, Understanding Fundamentalism and Evangelicalism (Grand Rapids, MI: Eerdmans, 1991), p. 1; on p. 103 he describes Carl McIntire as cantankerous.  Marsden is easily the most quoted expert on fundamentalism.
[12] Constitution on Church, also #50, using Hebrews 13:14; 11:10.
[13] See ch. 3 above, sec. 2 and n. 6.
[14] Note use in eschatology, #51, C. on Church.

who accept him.

Reputable Scripture scholars believe that some of Jesus' warnings about doctrinal deviations, flight from the world, etc. are His very words and go back to the earliest layers of the Gospel. The beatitudes which speak of persecution, insult and slander (Mt. 5:10-12) are incontestably Jesus' very words.[15]

Liberals notice especially the pessimism of the last books of the Bible: the Pastoral Epistles, Heb. 12:25-29; 2 Pt. 2; John's Epistles, and of course Revelation. But Gal 1:6-10; Rom. 1:18-32; 2 Cor. 12:19-21 are also negative and pessimistic, and they are much earlier. There are false teachers among us. Persecution by Rome (the secular and military power) made transforming the world very unlikely, and the flight from the world, much stronger.

We may not like these texts. Fundamentalists ask legitimately if it is right to ignore them.

Australian Scripture scholar William Loader looks at the issue of continuity and change. He wants to dialogue with fundamentalism about Jesus' attempts to update Jewish religion, and the early church's need to cope with adapting Jesus' teachings.[16]

The Sept. 27, 1986 issue of America was devoted entirely to

---

[15] See W.D. Davies, The Sermon on the Mount (Cambridge: The University Press, 1969, pp. 106-07; but contrasting, Marcel Dumais, O.M.I., Le Sermon sur la Montagne (Letouzey & Ane, 1995), pp. 45-46, 161.

[16] William Loader, Jesus and the Fundamentalism of His Day (Collingwood, Australia: Uniting Education, 1997). See his five page list of reading on reconciling continuity and change: 151-55.

"Fundamentalism." The Catholic archbishop of Hartford, CT, John Whealon, concentrated his article on explaining how the "Catholic Charismatic Renewal" persuaded him to lecture on "the Catholic Church and Biblical Fundamentalism."

The archbishop's attempt to reach out to those in the audience who were fundamentalists, especially regarding the Bible, is noteworthy. Perhaps most creative is the statement that "Catholics need to stop feeling inferior about the Bible," and his request that every parish have "a continuing Bible study group meeting every week and one scheduled 'Bible Mass' every Sunday.[17]

Whealon chaired the Ad Hoc Committee on Biblical Fundamentalism, which in 1987 produced the very important "A Pastoral Statement for Catholics on Biblical Fundamentalism." This short, nine page study promoted sound Biblical reading and alerted Catholics to the pitfalls of fundamentalist Bible claims.[18]

Biblical inerrancy is one of the major concerns of fundamentalists. Even Billy Graham is suspected of liberalism because of his attempts to move away from a narrow literalism.[19] Arnold notes that fundamentalists tend to ignore even the basics of Biblical understanding: "One frequently gets the impression that some Protestant sects believe in

[17] John F. Whealon, "Challenging Fundamentalism," America, Sept. 27, 1986, pp. 136, 138.
[18] National Conference of Catholic Bishops, A Pastoral Statement for Catholics on Biblical Fundamentalism (U.S. Catholic Conference, Washington, DC. 1987), also in Spanish. Fox cites much of it: pp. v-vi, Protestant Fundamentalism.
[19] See, for example, Foster, Streams of Living Water, pp. 208-15.

the absolute inerrancy of the Bible as given in the original English."[20]

Fox uses the old saw "the Bible is not a book of natural science. It tells

not how the heavens go but how to go to heaven."[21]

The Catholic struggle with fundamentalist approaches to the Bible

was fought within the structure of the "Pontifical Biblical Commission."

An easily accessible recent article outlines this fight: "Remnants of

Modernism in a Postmodern Age."[22]

## Historical Overview

In order to appreciate the appeal of fundamentalism today, and its

force, we need to briefly look at the history of Christianity, especially

when it was under extreme stress. We shall see the retreat to basics has

happened several times; it is no modern impulse.

Eusebius describes beautifully the Church's delight when

Constantine ceased the persecutions and the Christians emerged from

the catacombs (see ch. 5 below). But soon the Arian heresy threatened

to destroy Christianity from within. And from without, Islam from the

East and the Vikings from the North rather quickly reduced

Christianity's attempts to transform society. Christopher Dawson

explained the situation.

> On Candlemas Day 880 the whole northern army of the
> German kingdom, led by Bruno the Duke of Saxony, two

---

[20] Arnold, America, April 11, 1987, p. 301.

[21] Fox, Protestant Fundamentalism, p. 15.

[22] Dean Bechard, S.J., "Remnants of Modernism in a Postmodern Age: The Pontifical Biblical Commission's Centennial," America, Feb. 4, 2002, pp. 16-21.

bishops and twelve counts, was destroyed by the Danes in a great battle in the snow and ice at Ebersdorf on the Luneberg Heath. . . .

It is of these dark years that the chronicler of St. Vedast writes, "The Northmen cease not to slay and carry into captivity the Christian people, to destroy the churches and to burn the towns. Everywhere there is nothing but dead bodies—clergy and laymen, nobles and common people, women and children. There is no road or place where the ground is not covered with corpses. We live in distress and anguish before this spectacle of the destruction of the Christian people.". . .

Above all, this age destroyed the hope of a pacific development of culture which had inspired the leaders of the Church and the missionary movement and reasserted the warlike character of Western society which it had inherited from its barbarian past. Henceforward the warrior ethos, the practice of private war and the blood feud were as prevalent in Christian society as among its pagan neighbors.[23]

Is it any wonder that both Catholicism and Eastern Orthodoxy retreated into very fixed forms of worship? It was here that the Christian message was transmitted, and simple people became very attached to its stability. When the danger of the Northmen, of Islam (and later Communism) had passed, it would be very hard for people to leave the forms of worship which had given stability and hope to their lives.

## The Sixteenth Century Reformation

The Protestant Reformation certainly gave rise to a violent kind of fundamentalism. Luther's role in Muntzer's bloody revolt is still debated, but there is no doubt that the efforts of the radical right led to an

---

[23] Christopher Dawson, Religion and the Rise of Western Culture (Garden City, NY: Doubleday-Image, 1958), pp. 86-88.

attempt to return to fundamentals.[24] The Amish, Mennonite and Church of the Brethren (Dunkards) are descendants of these Anabaptists. The ones I met in Monroe County, West Virginia from 1982-91 are not generally considered fundamentalists today. But the stream they are related to started out in the 1520's as fundamentalist.

The Catholic Counter-Reformation also led to a noticeable rigidity in certain features of that Church. The Mass became frozen in Latin for most worshippers. Then the intellectual turmoil concentrated in the French Revolution caused a very negative attitude about European rationalism.

The growth of nationalism meant that Churches had to struggle to maintain the right to name their own bishops, without government interference. Napoleon kidnapped Pius VI and his most important cardinals, and attempted to block the papal election of 1799-1800.[25] When the young Pius IX, who was liberal leaning, suffered through the brutal assassination of his lay Premier, Pellegrino Rossi, on Nov. 15, 1848, he perhaps understandably shifted to a very uncooperative attitude towards liberals.[26]

Emperor Franz-Joseph of the Austro-Hungarian Empire attempted to exercise a veto during the papal election itself (1903).[27] Important

---

[24] Welch, Protestant Christianity, pp. 58-67.

[25] E.E.Y. Hales, Revolution and Papacy (Notre Dame, IN: Notre Dame University Press, 1966).

[26] E.E.Y. Hales, Pio Nono (New York, NY: Kenedy, 1954), p. 90.

[27] See J.M. Mayeur, "Rampolla Del Tindaro, Mariano," New Catholic Encyclopedia 12:76; also F. Maass, "Josephinism," New Catholic Encyclopedia 7: 1118-19.

administrative elements within Catholicism considered this another example of outside interference, and further retreated into a defensive, fundamentalist attitude.

## Catholic Fundamentalism, 1900-60

In chapter two above, I presented the general situation in American Christianity as it confronted the modern world at the beginning of the 20th century. The crisis which "blew apart the American Protestant Churches" (above, p. 55) also affected Catholicism and Eastern Orthodoxy. In the former, the problem is called "the Modernist-Integralist" crisis, with Modernism meaning liberalism, and Integralism fundamentalism. Scholars disagree about the exact relationship of Protestantism's crisis and Catholicism's crisis. Most agree they are at least "parallel." Anglican historian Alec Vidler treats the question well.[28] However the tonality may have differed, the outcome was the same: "a theological depression lasted until about 1945" (p. 55).

Pope Benedict XV found the bitterness between modernist and integralist to be so destructive that he forbade Catholics to call each other by these names.[29]

In the USA, the attempt by Catholic leaders to adapt to modern culture had an intriguing result: what some have called the phantom

---

[28] Alec Vidler, A Variety of Catholic Modernists (Cambridge: Cambridge University Press, 1970), p. 190.
[29] Walter H. Peters, Life of Benedict XV (Milwaukee, WI: Bruce, 1959), p. 108.

heresy "Americanism."[30] I will examine it more at length in ch. 5. Here we can affirm that Rome's action hindered any serious attempt by the American Catholic leadership to creatively address the challenge of the modern age, from about 1900 to 1945. It certainly made many American Catholics sympathetic to a fundamentalist mentality of retreat from intellectually challenging the many changes in society.

In the mid-1950's, prominent theologians such as Yves Congar, John Courtney Murray, Joseph Fuchs, and Stanislaus Lyonnet were all forbidden to write, or had some of their works withdrawn. Vatican II would find them in great prominence, especially the first two. As the Council began in 1962, few dreamed that their ideas (some of which did lack maturity) would find such an eager audience so quickly.[31]

The stream of renewal was never completely quashed: liturgical, Biblical, Patristic and lay movements all surfaced before Vatican II, and prepared the way for it.[32] One fundamentalist, the American Jesuit Leonard Feeney, was actually excommunicated by Rome in 1953 for interpreting literally the Patristic adage "Outside the Church, there is no salvation."[33] The Feeney experience did temper the drift towards fundamentalism.

---

[30] See especially Gerald P. Fogarty, S.J., The Vatican and the American Hierarchy from 1870 to 1945 (Collegeville, MN: Liturgical Press, 1982), pp. 115-90 (phantom, p. 188).

[31] For Congar, see chs. 1-3 above, pp. 12, 30, 66; for Fuchs, New Catholic Encyclopedia 19:145; Lyonnet, NCE 18:274-75; Murray, Donald E. Pelotte, S.S.S., John Courtney Murray (New York/Ramsey, NJ: Paulist, 1976).

[32] See the various entries in the New Catholic Encyclopedia, for example.

[33] Winthrop Hudson, Religion in America (1965 edition), p. 422; see Catechism (1994) for the soft interpretation, #'s 846-48.

# Protestant Fundamentalism, 1900-60

In 1920, "conservatives in the Northern Baptist Convention instituted a 'Fundamentals' conference to muster opposition to liberalism in that denomination. The term 'fundamentalist,' originated on this occasion," explains Marsden.[34]

Finding out exactly what the five fundamentals are is not that easy. Fox probably offers the best "summary." First, the literal inerrancy and infallibility of the Bible. Second, the Virgin birth and full deity of Christ. Third, the physical resurrection of Christ. Fourth, the atoning sacrifice of His death for the sins of the world. Fifth, Jesus' second coming in bodily form to preside at the Last Judgment.[35]

These five articles were drawn up at the Niagara Bible Conference of 1895, and between 1905-15, they were published and explained in twelve small volumes. Fox notes that "at least three million copies . . . were mailed free. . . . This had a tremendous influence at a time which was unacquainted with the mass media."[36]

The story of the bitter fights which broke out in each denomination is recounted in the histories of those denominations. Marsden observes that in the North, liberals tended to win and fundamentalists left to form separate denominations. In the South, fundamentalists tended to win,

---

[34] Marsden, Understanding Fundamentalism, p. 57.
[35] Fox, Protestant Fundamentalism, p. 13.
[36] Ibid.

and liberals simply left.[37]

An important step was taken in 1919, when "the militant World's Christian Fundamentalist Association" was established.[38] Billy Sunday's 1925 statement that "Our country is filled with a socialistic, communistic, radical, lawless, anti-American, anti-God, anti-marriage gang, and they are laying the eggs of rebellion and unrest, and we have some of them in our universities" sounded hauntingly relevant to America's editor in 1986. Sunday's opponents were "hog-jowled, weasel-eyed, sponge-columned, mush-faced, jelly-spined, pussy-footing, four-flushing, Charlotte-russe Christians."[39]

H. L. Mencken could quip "Heave an egg out a Pullman window, and you will hit a Fundamentalist almost anywhere in the United States today."[40] The 1928 presidential campaign of Catholic Al Smith mobilized fundamentalist forces. It was, in Marsden's view, "the last major appearance of fundamentalism," seemingly "the last hurrah for fundamentalism altogether." However, in a masterful analysis, he concludes:

> Their national organizations, either within denominations
> or in politics, declined; but vigor at the local level ensured
> that this segment of American Protestantism was one of the
> few that was growing during the 1930s. It was not until
> decades later, when fundamentalists and their evangelical

---

[37] Marsden, Understanding Fundamentalism, p. 74.

[38] Fox, Protestant Fundamentalism, p. 15.

[39] George W. Hunt, S.J., "Of Many Things, "America, Sept. 27, 1986, p. 128, noting that as recent as 1966, fundamentalism was supposed to be dead.

[40] H.L. Mencken, "Prejudices: Fifth Series," (first published New York, 1926 in The Discontent of the Intellectuals: A Problem of the Twenties, ed. Henry May (Chicago: Rand McNally, 1963), p. 30, cited by Marsden, Reforming Fundamentalism: Fuller Seminary, p. vii..

heirs reemerged in American life, that many observers noticed this growth or took it seriously.[41]

Gary Clabaugh shows how the sex education, McCarthyism, John Birch Society, and public education issues of the 1950's continued to foster the growth of fundamentalism, albeit in a behind-the-scenes manner.[42] The Foxfire series devoted one volume to religion, and the fundamentalism, especially of Appalachia, through the 1960's, was sympathetically presented.[43]

The Episcopalian fundamentalist splinter became the Reformed Episcopal Church; the Presbyterian, the Orthodox Presbyterian Church. The Church of Christ, (in 2001 one of the 25 largest Protestant denominations) was founded earlier. Now it benefited from the fundamentalist crisis.[44]

Hudson's treatment of fundamentalism is very complete:

> While Fundamentalism was a declining force throughout these years in the major denominations, it maintained itself in many local congregations, and expanded its influence through the formation of independent Bible churches and the capture of some of the smaller denominational bodies. A major source of its continuing strength was its ability to supply, through graduates of Bible schools or institutes strategically located throughout the nation, ministerial leadership to impoverished churches.[45]

Earlier he named Boston's Park Street Congregational Church,

---

[41] Marsden, Understanding Fundamentalism, p. 61.
[42] Gary K. Clabaugh, Thunder on the Right, The Protestant Fundamentalists (Chicago, IL: Nelson-Hall, 1974).
[43] Paul F. Gillespie, ed., Foxfire 7 (Garden City, NY: Anchor, 1973), especially pp. 21-22.
[44] For the ranking, see Yearbook of American and Canadian Churches 2002, pp. 11, 95.
[45] Winthrop S. Hudson, Religion of America (1965), p. 371.

pastor Harold J. Ockenga, and Philadelphia's Tenth Street Presbyterian Church, pastor Donald Grey Barnhouse, as two of the "many individual churches" which maintained fundamentalism and yet remained within more moderate denominations.[46]

## Protestant Fundamentalism, 1960 –

Karen Armstrong, "a distinguished British scholar and religious commentator," noted that fundamentalism began to mobilize in the 1960's, and by 1999 had become "part of the modern world," representing "a widespread disappointment, alienation, anxiety, and rage that no modern government can safely ignore."[47] The events of Sept. 11, 2001 may have intensified this judgement. Even though reasons may still be disputed about the growth of fundamentalism, and the relation of various sectors within it, we can at least look at some of the factors and personalities.

Marsden asserts that "wars are the catalysts of history."[48] He believes that World War I had a major impact on the growth of fundamentalism,[49] and he now factors in the Vietnam War as causing polarization within the broad evangelical spectrum, forcing moderates into the mainstream, and both increasing and isolating

---

[46] Ibid. p. 355. These national statistics (pp. 354-56) are very revealing.

[47] John A. Saliba, S.J., "Modernity vs. Fundamentalism," review of Karen Armstrong, <u>Battle for God</u> (New York, NY: Knopf, 2000), in <u>America</u> July 15-22, 2000, p. 23, citing her directly, p. 364. Armstrong starts in 1492, and has much valuable information on Jewish and Moslem fundamentalism, in addition to Christian. A former nun who calls herself a "freelance monotheist," she was interviewed by Faith L. Justice, "The Fundamentalist Battle for God," <u>Catholic Digest</u>, April 2002, pp. 84-90.

[48] Marsden, <u>Understanding Fundamentalism</u>, p. 50.

[49] Ibid, pp. 50-56.

fundamentalists.[50]

Political involvement developed especially around Jerry Falwell (a fundamentalist with evangelical sympathies) and Pat Robertson (an evangelical with fundamentalist sympathies). The attempt to influence the Republican Party was especially evident in the presidential elections of 1988 and 1992. Falwell himself has written "By 1976 the Fundamentalist Movement was so fragmented and diversified that it was impossible to describe it, categorize it, or even understand it."[51] In retrospect, the key word is diversify, for instead of fragmenting and disappearing, it was raising its controversial head in many, many groups and organizations where it had never before appeared.

Marsden observes that "After 1976 it became clear that a substantial evangelical, fundamentalist, and Pentecostal-charismatic constituency could be mobilized around these issues": anti-abortion, anti-pornography, anti-ERA, and symbolic religious issues such as school prayer.[52] It does not seem an exaggeration to state "the Christian Right stunningly captured the 1996 Republican platform committee."[53]

Fundamentalists who attended seminaries such as Fuller (Pasadena, CA) were exposed to the softening influence of broader

---

[50] Ibid, p. 74.
[51] Jerry Falwell, ed., The Fundamentalist Phenomenon (Garden City, NY: Doubleday, 1981), p. 143.
[52] Marsden, Understanding Fundamentalism, p. 95 (also pp. 78-79).
[53] Daniel A. Helminiak, "Christian (read Fundamentalist): A Case for Mistaken Identity," Ecumenical Trends 26 (Sept. 1997, #6): 1. He argues that fundamentalists must use the Council of Nicaea in order to affirm the divinity of Christ: historicity is needed.

evangelicalism.[54]  Experts cite "Garrison Keillor of Lake Wobegon fame as one well-known example" of "the struggle with fundamentalism . . . as a central event in their lives."[55]  One may also wonder if the popularity of Chaim Potok's novels during this time was also a sign of the fascination, and even sympathy for those experiencing the conflict between modernity and fundamentalism.  Potok's characters are Jews, but many other Americans found the novels telling.[56]

The most famous representative of academic and communal fundamentalism during this time was the American born couple Francis and Edith Schaeffer.  Catholic Archbishop Fulton Sheen, interviewed in Christianity Today, said:  "His summary of philosophical doctrines is one of the best that I have ever read, and I taught philosophy in graduate school for twenty-five years."[57]

Schaeffer's "L'Abri Fellowship" (from the French for shelter), spread from its birthplace (1955) in Huemoz, Switzerland, to many countries and several centers.  During its heyday in the 1970's, young people from all over the world flocked to its centers seeking fellowship.  I would place Schaeffer on the left wing of fundamentalism, especially after his attempt to make cause with Catholics on the abortion issue.  The videos "How Then Shall We Live" typify fundamentalism's approach to modern

---

[54] The classic work is George Marsden, Reforming Fundamentalism:  Fuller Seminary and the New Evangelicalism (Grand Rapids, MI:  Berdmans, 1987).

[55] Ibid, p. 11.

[56] Chaim Potok, The Chosen  (New York, NY:  Simon & Schuster, 1967); The Promise (New York, NY, Knopf, 1969); In the Beginning (New York, NY:  Knopf, 1975.)

[57] Cited by Thomas C. Reeves, America's Bishop (San Francisco, CA, 2001), p. 349, originally "An Interview with Fulton J. Sheen," Christianity Today, June 3, 1977, pp. 8-11.

culture: using its technology to attack much of its liberalism. Marsden

calls the videos "immensely popular."[58]

Another symbol of strict fundamentalism is Bob Jones University,

first established in 1926 in the Florida panhandle, moving to Tennessee

in 1933, and to Greenville, SC in 1946. Washington Post book reviewer

Jonathan Yardley described it in 1996 as "distinguished from other

American universities by its rigidly purist religious fundamentalism."[59]

Yardley agrees with author Mark Taylor Dalhouse in concluding that the

Jones' decision to have nothing to do with Billy Graham and Jerry

Falwell "left the Jones and their university as 'outsiders and the last

defenders of the true faith'."[60]

Many with fundamentalist sympathies recognized that stricter

fundamentalists were their own worst enemies (with friends like these,

who needs enemies?). So as Fox notes, they "have taken a more

sophisticated stance in seeking to shed the Fundamentalist badge by

identifying themselves with international conservative Protestant groups,

e.g., the World Evangelical Fellowship."[61] We can conclude today that

many strict fundamentalists are undergoing a moderating influence from

dialogue with more moderate evangelicals. And many moderate

evangelicals have strong fundamentalist sympathies because of this

---

[58] Marsden, Understanding Fundamentalism, p. 108 (also pp. 113, 183). See also Harry Winter, O.M.I., "Reluctant Ecumenist: Francis A. Schaeffer," Ecumenical Trends 14 (May, 1985, #5): 71-73.
[59] Jonathan Yardley, "Bob Jones U.: Cultural Reversity," Washington Post, Oct. 23, 1996, p. D2.
[60] Mark Taylor Dalhouse, An Island in the Lake of Fire (Athens, GA: University of Georgia Press, 1996), p. 115.
[61] Fox, Protestant Fundamentalism, p. 15.

contact.

During 1974, the celebrated Seminex crisis occurred in Missouri Synod Lutheranism. The synod (1974 membership 2,776,104) split between fundamentalists and more moderate conservatives, with the fundamentalists taking over Concordia Seminary (St. Louis) and the moderates withdrawing to "The Seminary in Exile," or Seminex. Arnold believes the moderates refused to "accede to a new fundamentalist agenda including biblical literalism."[62] A Missouri Lutheran author, however, demurred earlier: "there is no evidence of a general or lasting departure in the Synod from confessional Lutheranism to Fundamentalism."[63]

Armstrong documents the "severe setback" Protestant fundamentalism received in the "Television Scandals of 1987." Jimmy Swaggart, Jim and Tammy Faye Bakker, and the attempt by Jerry Falwell to rescue at least some of this ministry, are all detailed.[64] But in the end, it seems to have been more of a hiccup than a heart attack.

In "the closing days of 1990," David T. Morgan found Southern Baptist fundamentalists achieving "a definite victory," as they took over major administrative sections of the Convention, including seminaries.[65] Grady Cothen has an intriguing name for the increasing influence of the

---

[62] Arnold, "The Rise of Catholic Fundamentalism," America, April 11, 1987, p. 300; 1974 figure from the 1975 Yearbook of American and Canadian Churches, p. 60.

[63] Milton L. Rudnick, Fundamentalism and the Missouri Synod (St. Louis, MO: Concordia, 1966), p. 113.

[64] Armstrong, Battle for God, pp. 355-60.

[65] David T. Morgan, The New Crusades, The New Holy Land: Conflict in the Southern Baptist Convention, 1969-91 (Tuscaloosa, AL: University of Alabama Press, 1996), p. 106.

Southern Baptist administration: "catholicizing." This is his term for the movement away from the individual to the pastor and agencies.[66] As we saw in chapter one (p. 17, n. 22), people like former Southern Baptist John Claypool would consider this a legitimate development, and not necessarily evil. (A neo-orthodox analyst would see the individual and the governing body existing in creative tension.)

In 1991, a truly "monumental six-volume Fundamentalist Project"[67] sponsored by the American Academy of Arts and Sciences began to appear. Edited by Lutheran Martin Marty and Catholic R. Scott Appleby, the first and fifth concern us most directly. In their introduction, Marty and Appleby note the long, two year process which led to the first volume, and all the variations it revealed. They describe five ways in which fundamentalists fight, thereby distinguishing them from conservatives or traditionalists.[68] The first volume limited itself to describing fundamentalists across Christian and non-Christian religions. The fifth volume, appearing in 1995, attempted to find convergences.[69]

More important for its impact on American society was the Public Television and National Public Radio series originating from the first

[66] Grady C. Cothen, The New SBC (Macon, GE: Smyth & Helwys, 1995), especially ch. 5, "The Catholicizing of the Southern Baptist Convention," pp. 65-85.
[67] The description is Karen Armstrong's, The Battle for God, p. xi.
[68] Martin Marty and R. Scott Appleby, "The Fundamentalism Project: A User's Guide," Fundamentalisms Observed, (Chicago, IL: University of Chicago Press, 1991), pp. ix-x. A useful "glossary" is on pp. 843-50.
[69] Martin Marty and R. Scott Appleby, eds., Fundamentalisms Comprehended (Chicago, IL: University of Chicago Press, 1995).

volume, and written as The Glory and the Power. [70] A sober and easily digested presentation of fundamentalism marked a new level of analysis.

In its presentation of "The Christian School Movement," Martin and Appleby provide documentation for the claim that Christian school enrollment is about 700,000 students "in the late 1980s," with "as many as a hundred thousand fundamentalist children" being taught at home.[71]

In 1998, another English woman scholar, Harriet Harris produced a very valuable study for the impact of British conservatives and fundamentalists on the American scene.[72] The appendix "Comparative Fundamentalism" and "Glossary of Institutions" are highly recommended.[73]

Karen Armstrong's statistics are probably the most reliable up to 2001: "even through only 9 percent of Americans identified themselves as 'fundamentalists,' core tenets of Protestant fundamentalism were more widely held." Taking these from Marty-Appleby, she reproduced them:

44 percent believed that salvation comes only through Jesus Christ.
30 percent describe themselves as "born-again."
28 percent believe that every word of the Bible must be read literally.

---

[70]Martin Marty and R. Scott Appleby, The Glory and the Power: The Fundamentalist Challenge to the Modern World (Boston, MA: Beacon Press, 1992).
[71] Ibid, p. 74.
[72] Harriet A. Harris, Fundamentalism and Evangelicals (Oxford: Clarendon Press, (11998). See her presentation of Schaeffer: pp. 255-56; 260-62.
[73] Appendix, pp. 325-36; Glossary, pp. 337-39.

27 percent denied that the Bible could contain scientific and historical errors.[74]

Perhaps the most troubling observation concerning fundamentalism is made by Marsden. The more rigorous the fundamentalist, the less he is interested in revivalism, evangelism and outreach. The more angry and fearful one becomes, and obsessed with protecting the faith, the more difficult it becomes to share it.[75]

## Catholic Fundamentalism, 1960-

If the Vietnam War helped polarize Protestant Christianity in the USA, Catholics had an added challenge: their own polarization as the reforms mandated by Vatican II (1962-65) began, especially in worship. Pope John XXIII used the expression of opening the windows and letting in fresh air. I shall never forget the Oblate priest who huffed to me that a lot of bugs were coming in with the fresh air.

As shown above in the Scripture section (p. 89), Vatican II began with a strong sympathy towards fundamentalism. It ended with an opening to liberal Catholicism, as we shall see in ch. 5. One story told by Carmelite Mariologist Eamon Carrol concerns the request by Vatican II's Constitution on the Liturgy, the first document produced, to simplify worship practices. Some felt this meant a downgrading of the devotional

---

[74] Karen Armstrong, Battle for God, pp. 354-55, citing Marty and Appleby, Accounting for Fundamentalism, p. 20.
[75] Marsden, Understanding Fundamentalism, p. 110. See also Gillespie, Foxfire 7, p. 22.

prayer of the rosary. Carrol had been asked to help the US Catholic bishops write an instruction on Mary, including the rosary, which was published in 1973. He spent the year before traveling throughout the United States, preaching on Mary's role, and seeking input, especially from the pews. He related how he heard many times of the priest who went into the pulpit, pulled out his rosary beads, and ripped them apart, to demonstrate his interpretation of Vatican II's request. Then, with a smile, Carroll would tell us that he always asked the person "Did you actually see this yourself?" Not one person had actually seen it; it was always their cousin, uncle, etc who had witnessed it.[76]

Many Catholics, and many observers of religion in the 1970's felt that there were abuses in the reform, but that they were fairly minimal.

As local parishes simplified their worship, many threw out all the statues, paintings, altar railings, etc. so lovingly acquired over the years. The book title Bare Ruined Choirs captures the dismay felt by a significant number of Catholics, a dismay which made them at least sympathetic to Catholic fundamentalism.[77]

Vatican II began with the Catholic Church still suppressing liberal movements, still tilted towards a fear of the modern world, with rigidity in its government. Yet the powerful renewal forces mentioned in ch. 3

---

[76] Eamon Carrol, O.C., related this to the Oblate Community, Washington, DC during a retreat he gave in the early 1970's. For the Marian statement, see National Conference of Catholic Bishops, Behold Your Mother (Washington, DC: U.S. Catholic Conference, 1973).

[77] Garry Wills, Bare Ruined Choirs (Garden City, NY: Doubleday, 1972). The title is from Shakespeare's Sonnet 73, also used by the great Benedictine historian David Knowles, O.S.B. for his book describing Henry VIII's reform (NY: Cambridge, 1977).

were just below the surface, even within its government. As these burst forth, a significant number of Catholic leaders began to wonder if the fresh air of the changes which followed Vatican II was not sweeping away essentials.

The most articulate of these was the superior general of the Holy Ghost Congregation, and Archbishop, Marcel Lefebvre (1905-91). He served on the Central Preparatory Commission of Vatican II, and took a leading role in all four sessions of the Council. His touchstone was the Latin form of the Mass originating during the Council of Trent (1545-63). When the reforms of Vatican II swept this away, he began a series of protests which led to his excommunication by Rome on July 2, 1988.[78] However, his plea for the use of the Tridentine Mass as an option within Catholicism resulted in the growth of the use of the "Latin" or Traditional Mass (see above, ch. 1, p. 23). One may conclude that many who attend these Latin Traditional Masses are sympathetic to the conclusion that the Vatican II changes went too far, too fast, towards liberalism.

Both The Wanderer and the National Catholic Register extensively covered the efforts of the Catholic Church to end the schism. In January, 2002, one of the three bishops illicitly ordained by Lefebvre was reconciled, along with 26 priests and 28,000 laity.[79]

---

[78] For a clear explanation of the issues of the excommunication itself, see Peter J. Vere, "A Brief Canonical Examination of the SSPX Schism," The Catholic Answer 15 (May/June 2001, #2): 51-57.

[79] Pete Vere, "Why An Apostolic Administration?," The Wanderer, Feb. 21, 2002, pp. 4, 8; "Lefebvrite Traditionalist Schism in Brazil Ends," National Catholic Register, January 27-Feb. 2, 2002, p. 5, Jan. 13-19, 2002, p. 4.

When Father Francis Mannion presented five approaches to liturgy today, he observed about Catholic fundamentalism:

> The followers of Archbishop Marcel Lefebvre and the clerical Society of St. Pius X, which include a diverse American following, represent the more extreme expression of the restorationist agenda. They are unambiguously committed to the so-called Tridentine Mass. This wing of the restorationist agenda fundamentally rejects the ability of any pope to reform the Tridentine Mass and, for that reason, it objects in principle to the Missal of Paul VI.[80]

There does not seem to be a readiness to use the three year Scripture lectionary with the Tridentine Mass. The former one year lectionary used by Latin-rite Catholics certainly does not give the richness of Scripture readings. If dioceses are using the new Lectionary with the Tridentine Mass, they are certainly hiding it well.[81]

Scripture scholar and Catholic missiologist Eugene LaVerdiere alerted Catholics to something new and important in 1983.

> In recent years fundamentalism has been making significant inroads in the Roman Catholic Church, not that we have ever been altogether free of it. Never before, however, have we experienced it in its present form, where Catholics personally opt for a fundamentalist stance toward Scripture and its bearing on Christian life. A committed fundamentalism, as opposed to unconscious fundamentalist influence, is new for us. Having little experience with it, many do not know how best to approach it.[82]

The six panel pamphlet was widely distributed by bishops, religious order leaders, etc.

---

[80] M. Francis Mannion, "Agendas for Liturgical Reform," America, Nov. 30, 1996, p. 11.

[81] Correspondence with the Erie, PA diocese has gone unanswered.

[82] Eugene LaVerdiere, S.S.S., "Fundamentalism: A Pastoral Concern," Liturgical Press, Collegeville, MN, originally published in The Bible Today 21 (Jan. 1983, #1): 5-11 (underlining mine).

America's "Special Issue" on fundamentalism appeared in 1986 (above, pp. 87, 98).  Building explicitly on Marsden, editor George W. Hunt presented some of "the many paradoxes that characterize" fundamentalism.  Intensely patriotic, yet so individualistic that they are innately suspicious of government.  A millennialist confidence in God's triumph, yet exhibiting a palpable  fear about the survival of "Bible-based" Christianity.  So all reality is divided into "neat antitheses:  the saved and the lost, the holy and the unsanctified, the true and the false."[83]

In the same issue, college campus minister Richard Chilson angrily rejected an irenic approach to fundamentalists and called upon "Catholics and other Americans to perceive a Christian alternative to the Fundamentalist gospel of fear."  He presented five areas where this must be done:  First, the Gospel must be distinguished from American materialism.  Second, the emphasis on radical conversion is too close to wanting it all now.  (He does concede that the Catholic view of conversion has been too intellectual.)  Third, he wants a community context, concluding "the community is more crucial to Christianity than any book, including the Scriptures." (See Rolheiser in ch. 1, above, p. 12) Fourth, he wants "compassion" rather than "righteous tirades," and fifth, he rejects the opposing of anything not explicitly Christian as "of the

---

[83] George W. Hunt, S.J., "Of Many Things," America, Sept. 27, 1986, p. 128, citing historian Richard Hofstadter (no source, probably Anti-Intellectualism in American Life) for the antitheses.

devil."[84]

In the same issue, Martin Marty described the fundamentalism of the late 1980's:

> The "typical Fundamentalist" may be a simple lover of Jesus who runs the corner grocery. She may be at the keyboard of the computer at the next desk, an attractive, at-home-in-the-world person who expects Jesus' "soon" coming. He may be ready to witness about his "born-again" status or about the qualities of the Dallas Cowboys. The Fundamentalist is at home in the science class and in the evening seeks out a campus cell devoted to a doctrine of biblical inerrancy that contends that every scriptural statement that bears on science is accurate. She is married to a soul partner, and together they attend church, want to bring up their children in the faith and are preoccupied with an American moral crisis.[85]

1987 was the year of the US Catholic Bishops document on Biblical Fundamentalism (above, p. 91) and 1988, Karl Keating's first book (above, p. 88).

O'Meara's short work appeared in 1990, and incorporated many of the earlier Catholic studies. He too felt it was time for a wake up call: "In Florida it is estimated that five Catholics enter fundamentalist churches every day."[86] He ventured that the major reason for the explosion of fundamentalism is that "Americans are tired of change: numbed by the past twenty-five years of rapid change in every area of life: frightened by change which leads only to more change." He

---

[84] Richard W. Chilson, C.S.P., "A Call to Catholic Action," America, Sept. 27, 1986, pp. 148, 150, based on his book Full Christianity (Mahwah, NY: Paulist, 1985).
[85] Martin E. Marty, "Modern Fundamentalism," America, Sept. 27, 1986. p. 133.
[86] Thomas F. O'Meara, O.P., Fundamentalism: A Catholic Perspective (Mahwah, NJ, 1990), p. 7, using LaVerdiere, Whealon, Arnold, etc., and giving a good survey of other authors.

concluded a long description of change:

> Fundamentalism is in the air. People respond to fundamentalist theologies and politics. The televised crowds are happy with either an upbeat and simple message, or with an apocalyptic prediction.[87]

> (Remember that he wrote this 11 years before Sept. 11, 2001.)

O'Meara explains very clearly that, in contrast to Protestants who exaggerate the Bible or baptism in the Holy Spirit, and Muslims, who dispute over the black rock at Mecca, Catholics "will find their fundamentalism in (1) sacramental things and in (2) church authority." All fundamentalists, O'Meara feels, exaggerate something central.[88]

In 1991 Marty-Appleby's Fundamentalism Project devoted a must-read chapter to "Roman Catholic Traditionalism and Activist Conservatism in the United States." William D. Dinges, a professor of religion and religious education at the Catholic University of America, wrote the first half, explaining why he chose traditionalism over fundamentalism, and the parallels and interactions.[89] His explanation of Archbishop Lefebvre's group, and the Vatican's attempts to draw away a significant portion (the 1988 Society of St. Peter) is probably the most accessible summary of this sad matter.[90] Dinges also credits the change factor, noting "with the Second Vatican Council, however, change in

---

[87] O'Meara, pp. 10-11.
[88] O'Meara, p. 24. See his explanation for "orthodoxy," and "neo-orthodoxy," p. 23.
[89] William D. Dinges, "Roman Catholic Traditionalism," Fundamentalisms Observed, eds. Martin E. Marty and R. Scott Appleby, pp. 78-101; viii-ix.
[90] Dinges, pp. 66-68, 74-78, 97-98.

Catholic ecclesiology and theology accelerated dramatically."[91]

James Hitchcock, an articulate conservative professor of history at St. Louis University, wrote the second half, "Catholic Activist Conservatism in the United States." He begins by situating demonstrations for integration and peace of the 1960's with the pro-life demonstrations of the 1980's and since. He then proceeds to show, in my opinion, that conservativism within Catholicism can be compared to evangelicalism with Protestantism. He reserves, as does Dinges, traditionalism as an extreme form of evangelicalism. Such conservative Catholic groups as Catholics United for the Faith, Opus Dei, Blue Army and many more are succinctly explained, and shown where they stop short of separatist traditionalism.[92] His presentation of the Catholic Charismatic Movement from the conservative viewpoint is especially intriguing.[93]

In 1992, the influential series Concilium devoted an issue to fundamentalism, including Eastern Orthodox, Jewish and Islamic. Jesuit sociologist John Coleman observed "global fundamentalism, expanding since the mid-1970s, took most sociologists by almost total surprise."[94] Coleman notes that "sometimes it is difficult to draw neat lines between fundamentalists and more nuanced traditionalists or

---

[91] Ibid, p. 80.
[92] James Hitchcock, "Catholic Activist Conservatism in the United States," Fundamentalisms Observed, pp. 101-41; Dinges, 100.
[93] Hitchcock, ibid, pp. 125-26.
[94] John Coleman, S.J., "Global Fundamentalism: Sociological Perspectives," Fundamentalism as an Ecumenical Challenge (London: SCM, 1992), Concilium, 1992, Vol. 3, eds. Hans Kung and Jurgen Moltmann, p. 36.

conservatives. This ambiguity gives to fundamentalism a power beyond the radical fringe groups which espouse it wholly."[95]

Yet Coleman also believes that "frequently, it may be the genuine conservatives of the religious tradition who serve as the most powerful defense against fundamentalists, since they see the extent to which fundamentalists are really 'innovators' and not mere conservatives."[96]

The 1994 volume of Marty-Appleby contained an extremely important chapter on the Catholic movement "Comunione e Liberazione." Italian sociologist Dario Zadra gives the best summary available of the way this "traditionalist" movement has matured.[97]

In 2000, Archbishop Alex Brunett experienced first hand the fundamentalism of some Eastern Orthodox monks. He related how the North American Catholic and Orthodox bishops' dialogue met on the Island of Crete, with several of the Catholic going to Mount Athos in Greece with two Orthodox bishops before the scheduled meeting.

> The first day was filled with courteous receptions at the Monastery of Iviron perched high above the Aegean Sea. Although the Orthodox members of our delegation were welcomed warmly and fondly embraced, the Roman Catholic members were not offered as much as a handshake. We asked to participate in the singing of the Divine Office but were told that the most we would be able to do was to sit in the dark narthex where we would be able neither to see nor hear. Walking across the courtyard from the church toward the refectory, one of the monks peering at me dressed in my

---

[95] Ibid, p. 38.
[96] Ibid, giving examples from Catholicism, and Southern Baptists, p. 70.
[97] Dario Zadra, "Comunione e Liberazione: A Fundamentalist Idea of Power," Accounting for Fundamentalisms, pp. 124-48. See also Ammerman, ibid, p. 15. In 1991, James Hitchcock had noticed CL's importance: Fundamentalisms Observed, pp. 123-24. See ch 1 above.

black cassock with red buttons, shouted, "Cardinali!
Heretiki!" You look like a Cardinal. You are a heretic!
    Fortunately, as our time on Mount Athos passed and as
word of our presence spread from monastery to monastery,
as well as our prayerful respect became known, the attitude
slowly began to change.[98]

The reaction to rapid change may be seen in the popularity of the

Aubrey-Maturin 20 volume series by Patrick O'Brian. In several of the

episodes, he popularized the Spanish greeting of the 19th century "May

no new thing arise."[99] This series, with its emphasis on the essential

conservatism of the British navy, appealed very much to the spirit of the

1990's (its description of the worship of Anglican, Catholic, and the more

esoteric British sects is priceless).

The solution of Ratzinger, who served as a theologian during the

Council itself, is not to "simply hammer away at fundamentalism—whose

definition keeps getting broader and broader," but to offer a "positive way

to faith." There is, he believes, a very normal and Biblical thirst "for

simplicity and certainty," which only "becomes dangerous when it leads

to fanaticism and narrow-mindedness."[100]

Fox shows the sympathy many Catholics have for fundamentalism.

"While they may not preach the full Gospel they are in fact preaching a

fuller Gospel than those tinted with Modernism, who teach while wearing

---

[98] Alex J. Brunett, "Harvesting the Past, Planting for the Future: Our Pilgrimage Together," Ecumenical Trends 30 (Feb. 2001, #2): 4/20. This speech was the Sixth Paul Wattson Lecture, and delivered at St. Mary's University, Halifax, Nova Scotia, Nov. 6, 2000. It is well worth reading in its entirety (pp. 1/17-11/27).
[99] For example, Patrick O'Brian, Wine-Dark Sea (New York, NY: Norton, 1993), p. 130; Letter of Marque (1992), p. 155; Ionian Mission (1997), p. 319.
[100] Joseph Ratzinger, Salt of the Earth, (San Francisco, CA: Ignatius Press, 1997), p. 137.

the mask of 'Catholicism'."[101]

## Convergence of Protestant and Catholic Fundamentalism

Some fundamentalist groups are definitely making common cause across the Protestant-Catholic divide. Francis Schaeffer's efforts have been mentioned above. At least one Catholic archbishop remembers the appointment Schaeffer made with him, to promote the videos "How Then Shall We Live?"[102]

Helminiak singled out the Christian Coalition's attempt "to incorporate conservative Catholics" by the "Catholic Alliance."[103] Certainly not all fundamentalists are interested in politics, but it does seem that a growing number recognize sympathies in other denominations and religions.

Observers of fundamentalism in all religions probably find a Bob Thaves "Frank and Ernest" cartoon illustrative of fundamentalism's bold attitude.[104] On the far right, a tiny fish, mouth open, is ready to swallow a number of progressively larger fish, right up to the tip of the food chain. Frank says to Ernest: "You've got to admire his spunk."

One trait, which was absent in Catholicism until recently, now unites both Catholics and Protestants: the shopping mentality.

---

[101] Robert Fox, Protestant Fundamentalism, p. 4.
[102] Interview, Winter with Archbishop Francis Bible Schulte when the latter was bishop of Wheeling-Charleston, WV, Nov. 3, 1987.
[103] Daniel Helminiak, "Christian (read Fundamentalist): A Case for Mistaken Identity," Ecumenical Trends 26 (Sept., 1997, #8) 1/113.
[104] See Keating, Catholicism and Fundamentalism, p. 340 for a significant quote from Hiliare Belloc to illustrate the cartoon.

Ammerman summarizes it:

> Charismatic Catholic prayer meetings and Full Gospel
> (Protestant) lunches may by frequented by the same
> converts, either con-currently or in serial fashion, as the
> population shops about among various religious visions of
> reform. . . . many local believers still move rather casually
> across boundaries their leaders would draw more
> emphatically.[105]

One of the Christian aphorisms which fundamentalists in every

denomination rely on is "The Holy Spirit and I make a majority." James

Hastings Nichols noted the ability to compartmentalize.[106] We might

state that some fundamentalists compartmentalize their faith in one

section, and their ability to work with modern technology in another

section. Other fundamentalists refuse to compartmentalize, and reject

modern ways. A third group finds that compartmentalizing puts them on

the slippery slope, especially to neo-orthodoxy or catholicism, and they

follow that direction.

Martin Marty notes very accurately that "the rise of technology led

more liberal thinkers—from Buber in Judaism, Berdyaev in Orthodoxy,

Maritain in Catholicism, Tillich in Protestantism, and almost everyone

else—to be wary."[107] Does the computer run us, or we run the

computer? A growing number of fundamentalists are eager for a sound

spirituality which counters the pitfalls of modern technology.

Marsden's critique is quite thorough, praising the right kind of

---

[105] Nancy T. Ammerman, "Accounting for Christian Fundamentalism," Marty-Appleby 4:162.
[106] James Hastings Nichols, Corporate Worship in the Reformed Tradition (Philadelphia, PA: Westminster, 1968), p. 135, calling it as Puritans and Pietists did it "surprisingly effective in practice."
[107] Martin E. Marty, "Modern Fundamentalism," America, Sept. 27, 1986, p. 135.

individualism: "some of the most cohesive nonethnic communities in America" are fundamentalistic.[108]  And as noted above, his most damming observation concerns the downgrading of evangelism by the stricter fundamentalists (above, p. 107).

The appearance of Marty-Appleby's fifth and final volume in 1995 provided many insights on the convergence of various fundamentalisms. General statistics showed the continual decline in the membership of mainline Protestantism (over several decades) and the "sharp increase" in the size of denominations which included a majority of fundamentalists.[109]  The authors could now look at "the Second Public Emergence" of Protestant fundamentalism in the USA (late 1970s to the present) with a little more perspective.[110]

The most valuable insights are the "five ideological and four organizational properties of the 'family'," of fundamentalism. Ideologically, all fundamentalists react strongly to the marginalization of religion; they are selective; they firmly divide the world into good and evil; they are absolutist and inerrant, and they expect victory (millennialism and messianism).[111]

Organizationally, fundamentalists consist of the faithful remnant; they have sharp boundaries; insist on authoritarian organization, and

---

[108]Marsden, Understanding Fundamentalism, p. 115, also the "paradox" of its anti-intellectualism, especially as regards technology.
[109] Gabriel A. Almond, et. al, "Explaining Fundamentalisms," Marty-Appleby, Fundamentalisms Comprehended (Chicago: University of Chicago Press, 1995), 434-35.
[110] Ibid, pp. 451-52.
[111] Ibid, pp. 3, 405-07.

strict, communal behavioral.[112]  Two chapters  on how fundamentalists

narrate their own story are very insightful.[113]  There are also valuable

updates on fundamentalism in Appalachia,[114] Southern Baptist data,[115]

and the two kinds of Catholic traditionalism:  Archbishop Lefebvre[116] and

Comunione e Liberazione.[117]

Jurgen Moltmann perhaps was too irenical when he wrote:

> We shall have to live with fundamentalism—against us,
> alongside us, and even in us.  The liberation of
> fundamentalists for openness to the future of God and the
> world remains a task for theology and the church.[118]

When Marty and Appleby began the Fundamentalism Project, they

observed:

> . . . the voices of the fundamentalists. . . are challenges
> to those who have held non-and counter fundamentalist
> understandings of reason, practice and politics.  They help
> force critical examination of beliefs and presuppositions and
> thus in a way are a mirror for the Western academy, a
> window toward the future to be shared by
> antifundamentalists and fundamentalists alike.[119]

Their final words for the entire project were a little more critical:

> For fundamentalisms are caught in a debilitating
> paradox.  As long as they remain fixed in the enclave culture
> and mentality that nurture them, fundamentalists are fated

---

[112] Ibid, pp. 407-08, with pp. 409-14 examining how the organizational and ideological interrelate. There are many valuable charts:  pp. 410, 414-15, 430, 432, 446, 478-79.

[113] James L. Peacock and Tim Pettyjohn, (ch. 4), "Fundamentalisms Narrated:  Muslim, Christian and Mystical," pp. 115-34; Wayne C. Booth, (ch. 15) "The Rhetoric of Fundamentalist Conversion Narratives," pp. 367-395.

[114] Ibid, pp. 120-26.

[115] Ibid, p. 435.

[116] Ibid, pp. 422, 476-77.

[117] Ibid, 463-64.

[118] Jurgen Moltmann, "Fundamentalism and Modernity," Fundamentalism as an Ecumenical Challenge (Concilium, 1992, #3) (London:  SCM, 1992), p. 11.

[119] Marty-Appleby, Fundamentalisms Observed, p. xiii.

to be no more than disruptive and relatively influential dissenting minorities; yet once they exit the enclave, mentally or otherwise, they find that their fundamentalist religious ardor quickly yields to the pragmatic, compromising strategies of a world not of their liking—the impure, very real world outside the enclave.[120]

I began this chapter by distinguishing between our instinct for preservation of our family, country and faith, on the one hand and modern fundamentalism, with all of its separatist tendency, on the other. After September 11, 2001 the formula used by Dinges which distinguishes between "a fundamentalist orientation—which may be a latent ethos in any religious tradition—and a separatist fundamentalist movement" is extremely important.[121] For the next few decades, any serious Christian will have to deal with both the orientation and the movement. And may the Holy Spirit help us!

---

[120] Gabriel A. Almond, Emmanuel Sivan, R. Scott Appleby, "Politics, Ethnicity, and Fundamentalism," Fundamentalisms Comprehended, p. 504.

[121] William D. Dinges, "Roman Catholic Traditionalism," Fundamentalisms Observed, p. 99 (underlining is italics in the original).

## Overview

With the election of John F. Kennedy as President of the United States in November, 1960, and the Second Vatican Council of 1962-65, Catholic liberal Christianity exploded on the religious scene after a half century of silence. With the election of Bill Clinton as president in November, 1992, Protestant liberal Christianity took on new life, after twelve years of Reagan-Bush conservatism. Catholic liberals converged with Protestant liberals.

The influence of the Bible Belt on the election of George W. Bush in November, 2002 is commonly acknowledged, and documented in our booklet on ch. 4. The Republican Party's recapturing of the presidency, and the events of September 11, 2001, seems to have left liberal Christianity on the defensive. But Bush's razor thin victory means liberal Christianity is still very strong.

The liberal stream may be viewed as the most dynamic, creative, and frustrated of the five streams (Conservatives always think they are winning; liberals always think they are losing: see "Note on Conservatives and Liberals," above, pp. 86-88). Thomas O'Meara vindicates a genuine Christian liberalism:

> "Liberal" is related to the word "liberty," freedom. To be liberal is to be free: with money, with ideas, with plans for changing things. Every political party, every philosophy or theory of art, every theology has a liberal side attracting men

and women who are more open to change then to remaining
in a stable, conserving stance.[1]

He concludes "Without some liberalism a church dies of entropy."

But he also finds that "Liberal theology in its unbridled form ends up as

psychology," even becoming "fundamentalist," when it denies that any

other approach is legitimate.[2] Liberalism as a tendency is absolutely

necessary; liberalism as an obsession fragments and leads to anarchy

and worse.

Perhaps Claude Welch gives the best short description of liberal

Christianity, summarizing its five themes: open-mindedness, respect for

science, skepticism about achieving certain knowledge of ultimate reality,

emphasis on the principle of continuity, and confidence in the future of

humanity.[3] (Although Welch is writing specifically about Protestant

liberalism, I believe his themes apply to liberals in every religion).

Another feature of liberalism is that it always seems to be "the

scattered left," in contrast to conservatism, "the solid right."[4] Statistics

bear this out. Carl F.H. Henry cited a 1957 sampling of the theological

convictions of American clergy: "14 per cent identified themselves as

liberal, 12 per cent as neo-orthodox, and 74 per cent as either

conservative or fundamentalist."[5]

---

[1] Thomas F. O'Meara, O.P., Fundamentalism: A Catholic Perspective (Mahwah, NJ: Paulist, 1970), p. 77.
[2] Ibid, p. 78.
[3] Claude Welch and John Dillenberger, Protestant Christianity (NY: Scribner, 1954), pp. 211-14.
[4] John W. Healey, "Symbols Are Not 'Just Symbols'," America, Dec. 23-30, 2000, p. 16, probably quoting Bernard Lonergan, S.J.
[5] Carl F.H. Henry, "Evangelicals and Ecumenism," Christianity Today, May 27, 1966, p. 11.

Protestant liberalism flourished in the early 1960's as neo-orthodoxy faded. Catholic liberalism peaked in 1976, and then declined along with Protestant liberalism. As the 21st century began, liberal Christianity became more militant, perhaps spurred by its strong foe, fundamentalism.

First we shall examine the way liberal Christianity uses Scripture, then glance at its appearance at important moments in Church History (usually peaceful moments), before we look at its fascinating life during the last century in the USA.

## Scripture Model of the Church and Its Implications

Liberals are suspicious of institutions, and instinctively relate to freedom and flexibility. What model of the Church is the most flexible? The Holy Nation of I Pt 2:9-10: "You, however, are 'a chosen race, a royal priesthood, a holy nation, a people he claims for his own to proclaim the glorious works' of the One who called you from darkness into his marvelous light."6 A nation can change its structures of government and still remain a nation. Consider France of the Monarchy of Louis XVI, of the Revolution, of Napoleon, etc. The same nation, but very different forms of government. This is the most flexible of all images, and relies on structures the least, which pleases liberals.

Fundamentalists emphasize Scripture passages about <u>flight</u> from

---

6 Bishop's Committee of the Confraternity of Christian Doctrine, <u>New American Bible</u> (Camden, NJ: Thomas Nelson, 1971), p. 1355, citing Ex. 19:6.

the world, and its sin, conflict, evil and false prophets. Liberals emphasize Jesus' words to <u>transform</u> the world, to be salt, light, and leaven (Mt. 5:13-16; 13:33). Paul's boldness at the Areopagus catches the liberal imagination.[7]

As we noted above in ch. 3 (p. 63), critics such as H.R. Niebuhr accused Protestant liberals of jettisoning the unpleasant half of a number of Gospel tensions. "Christ without a cross" was verified recently by Associated Press writer Richard Ostling. "The cross is spurned by Christian liberals Rita Nakashima Brock and Rebecca Ann Parker," the former a Harvard Divinity researcher who has chaired the joint global ministries board of the Christian Church (Disciples of Christ) and United Church of Christ, and the latter a United Methodist minister and president of the Unitarian Universalist seminary in Berkely, CA. They were joined by Catholic Scripture scholar "leftist John Dominic Crossan." The argument grew in the aftermath of September 11, 2001 and the "cross of fused beams found in the rubble of the World Trade Center."[8]

Liberals have an enormous problem with Scripture. So much of it seems time conditioned, not only in the Old Testament but even in the New. Protestant neo-orthodoxy found ways to interpret these passages without abandoning them. Liberals tend to throw them out. When Catholics devised a three-year Sunday lectionary (quickly adapted by

---

[7] For a thorough examination, see Dean Flemming, "Contextualizing the Gospel in Athens," <u>Missiology</u> 30 (April, 2002, #2): 199-214.

[8] Richard N. Ostling, Associated Press, "The Debate Over the Religious Meaning of the Cross," <u>Buffalo News</u>, March 23, 2002, p. D1.

Protestant main-line Churches), and revised the readings for the Divine

Office which all priests and many laity pray each day, offensive passages

such as Ps. 137:7-9 ("Happy the man who shall seize and smash you

little ones against the rock!") were dropped.   Rather than eliminate such

passages from the daily or Sunday texts, most other Christians find ways

to explain them.[9]

It does seem odd that the passage in Mt. 10:34-36 regarding Jesus

bringing not peace but division is omitted in the Sunday Lectionary (12th

and 13th Sundays in Ordinary Time, Year A).  Norman Bonneau, in his

explanation of the reasons for the lectionary's selectivity, does not

mention this passage.[10]  Is it a coincidence that liberals prefer tranquility

over division, and have difficulty coping with war, sin, and bloodshed?

In a recent discussion of how uncomfortable a clerical culture (and

some sophisticated ones, too?) is talking about sex, an alert user of the

Divine Office noticed that the very sexually blunt second half of Ezekiel

16:7 is omitted from that passage for Friday, 24th Week in Ordinary

Time.  He wondered if it were a sign of squeamishness "about the

sacredness of sexuality in marriage."[11]  I suspect it is also a liberal fear

that people cannot work out for themselves the limitations of Scripture

passages.

In 1986, Leonard Sweet, while discussing the future of liberal

---

[9] Artur Weiser, The Psalms (London:  SCM Press, 1962), pp. 796-97.
[10] Normand Bonneau, O.M.I., The Sunday Lectionary (Collegeville, MN:  Liturgical Press, 1998), pp. 49-51.
[11] Herbert P. Ely, "Letters," American, July 29-Aug. 5, 2002, pp. 28, 30.

Protestantism, stated: "The rediscovery of the lectionary has returned the Bible to many sanctuaries, but it is an ecclesiastically edited Bible, a 'reader's digest' scripture that omits difficult passages and seriously mangles the Old Testament."[12]

Both Catholic and Protestant liberals flinch at the passages of the Bible which show their links to an earlier culture. I have often wondered if Niebuhr were alive today, would he have added a fifth stroph to his famous contrast: Liberals hold to a Bible without real relevance to modern times?

## Historical Overview

Even before the persecutions ended, Justin Martyr was boldly attempting to explain Christianity to the emperor and all pagans.[13] He epitomizes the liberal belief that reason and grace can overcome all.

When Constantine ended the persecutions, Christianity had the peace it needed to challenge the culture. Eusebius describes the new atmosphere.

> When this had been done, it was as if a light had suddenly blazed out of a dark night. In every city, churches were thronged, congregations crowded, and rites duly performed. All the unbelieving heathen were astonished at the wonder of so great a transformation and hailed the Christians' God as alone great and true. Among our own people, those who had valiantly contended through the ordeal of persecution again enjoyed freedom with honor, but

---

[12] Leonard Sweet, "Can a Mainstream Change Its Course?," Liberal Protestantism (New York, NY: Pilgrim Press, 1986), eds. Robert S. Michaelson and Wade Clark Roof, p. 238.

[13] Justin Martyr, First Apology in Defense of the Christian; two excerpts are used in the Liturgy of the Hours (New York: Catholic Book Publishing Co., 1976) 3:694-95; 719-21.

those whose faith had been anemic and their souls in turmoil eagerly sought healing, begging the strong to extend the right hand of rescue and imploring God to be merciful to them.  Then, too, the noble champions of godliness, released from their misery in the mines, returned to their own homes, rejoicing and beaming as they went through every city, exuding an indescribable delight and confidence.  Crowds of men went on their way, praising God with hymns and psalms in the middle of the thoroughfares and public squares.  Those who a little earlier had been prisoners, cruelly punished and driven from their homelands, now regained their own hearths with smiles of elation, so that even those who had thirsted for our blood saw this unexpected wonder and shared our joy at what had happened.[14]

Confidence and optimism do pervade "the great Patristic enterprise which led to the creation of the Christian intellectual and cultural world," as Joseph Komonchak describes this achievement.[15]

When Pope Gregory the Great instructed Augustine not to force the English to accept all the Roman practices, but to adapt when advantageous, he was using the liberal instinct of creativity.

The heathen temples of these people need not be destroyed, only the idols which are to be found in them. . . . If the temples are well built, it is a good idea to detach them from the service of the devil, and to adapt them for the worship of the true God . . . And since the people are accustomed, when they assemble for sacrifice, to kill many oxen in sacrifice to the devils, it seems reasonable to appoint a festival for the people by way of exchange.  The people must learn to slay their cattle not in honour of the devil, but in honour of God and for their own food; when they have eaten and are full, then they must render thanks to the giver of all good things.  If we allow them these outward joys, they

---

[14] Eusebius of Caesarea, Eusebius, The Church History, trans. Paul L. Maier (Grand Rapids, MI: Kregel, 1999), Book 9, 311, 1 (p. 322).

[15] Joseph A. Komonchak, "Vatican II and the encounter between Catholicism and Liberalism," Catholicism and Liberalism (New York, NY:  Cambridge University Press, 1994), eds. R. Bruce Douglass and David Hollenbach, S.J., p. 86.  This extremely important book is described further below, p. 138.

are more likely to find their way to the true inner joy. . . . It is doubtless impossible to cut off all abuses at once from rough hearts, just as the man who sets out to climb a high mountain does not advance by leaps and bounds, but goes upward step by step and pace by pace.[16]

When Pope Adrian II encouraged Cyril and Methodius to use Slavonic instead of Latin on their missionary efforts in Eastern Europe, they were using the liberal instinct of creativity.[17] When Thomas Aquinas attempted "to meet, confidently and discriminatingly, the challenge to that world represented in the medieval period by the introduction of Aristotelian philosophy and Arab science," he was using the liberal instinct of creativity. Thomas was considered the liberal of his day, and paid the usual price of bureaucratic rejection.[18]

As Welch notes, Renaissance humanism shifted the focus from God and His Church, to "the greatness and nobility of man."[19] Soon Socinius would reject the Trinity, and become the ancestor of New England Unitarianism. Liberals, in their attempts to make Christianity understandable, are always exposed to the peril of rejecting key Christian beliefs such as the Trinity of God and the divinity of Christ. The "left

---

[16] Gregory the Great, Letter of July 18, 601, reproduced by Bede, Ecclesiastical History of the English Nation, Bk, 1:30, and cited by Stephen Neill, A History of Christian Missions (Baltimore, MD: Penguin Books, 1964), The Pelican History of the Church, vol. 6, pp. 68-69. Neill notes that the letter was not addressed to Augustine directly, but to the abbot Mellitus, "who was on his way to Britain and was instructed to convey the contents to Augustine."

[17] Neill, A History of Christian Missions, pp. 86-87; Andrew F. Walls, The Missionary Movement in Christian History (Maryknoll, NY: Orbis, 1996) recommends A.P. Vlasto, "The Mission of Ss. Cyril and Methodios and its Aftermath in Central Europe," in G.L. Cuming, The Mission of the Church and Propagation of the Faith (Cambridge, 1970), pp. 1-16.

[18] Komonchak, Catholicism and Liberalism, p. 86. For an application to medieval society, see Paul E. Sigmund, "Catholicism and liberal democracy," ibid, pp. 219-21.

[19] Welch, Protestant Christianity, p. 9.

wing" of the Reformation does seem to lead to modern liberalism.[20]

On the other hand, Princeton seminary's theologian of worship alerts us to the need which Unitarians and other liberals fulfill:

> Again and again it has been needed to liberate deeper forms of Christianity, Protestant and Catholic alike, from obscurantism, idolatry, sectarianism, and intolerance. There are, for example, serious problems of conscience for many in the liturgical use of the Catholic creeds, problems that are not solved by the sophisticated interpretations of the theologians. The health of the church has often been served by the Unitarian demand for intellectual integrity.[21]

During the 17-18th centuries' "Rites Controversy" among the Jesuits in China, Rome issued a remarkable statement:

> What could be more absurd than to carry France, Spain, or Italy, or any part of Europe into China? It is not this sort of things you are to bring but rather the Faith, which does not reject or damage any people's rites and customs, provided these are not depraved.[22]

In our own times, the code word of "inculturation" has been developed, especially by missionaries, to discuss how to distinguish what is "depraved" from what should be taken from newer cultures and even classic religions, and used by Christianity.[23] Liberals have been at the forefront of this effort.

Unfortunately, the convergence of political and religious conservatism and even fundamentalism during the 18th-19th centuries

---

[20] For Unitarian worship in England and the USA, see James Hastings Nichols, Corporate Worship in the Reformed Tradition (Philadelphia, PA: Westminster, 1968), pp. 138-41.

[21] Ibid, p. 151.

[22] Cited in David J. Bosch, Transforming Mission (Maryknoll, NY: Orbis, 1993), p. 449; see also Neil, A History of Christian Missions, pp. 88-94.

[23] Bosch, Transforming Mission, pp. 447-57.

doomed such inculturation in Catholic missionary efforts. As Bosch

notes, Protestant missionaries only "appeared" to be different; they

unwittingly subordinated the Gospel not to magisterial authority in

Rome, but to "the presuppositions of Euro-American culture."[24]

William Warren Sweet puts it very bluntly when he describes

English-speaking Protestant Christianity coming to the New World.

"With hardly an exception, the leaders in the establishment of the

American colonies were liberal and even radical in both their religious

and political views," He notes that many were poor, "easily lured by

radical ideas," and that persecuted radicals of non-English background

such as Mennonites, Dunkers, Moravians and Schwenkfelders were

welcomed.[25]

When the colonists established seminaries, they would soon notice

the impact of a German theologian sometimes called the Father of

Protestant liberalism, Friedrich Schleiermacher (1768-1834). All agree

that Schleiermacher presented a powerful argument for individual

religious experience, not doctrine in creeds or the Bible, as the starting

point of religion. His <u>Speeches on Religion to its Cultured Despisers</u>[26]

has become almost a slogan by liberal Christians in their attempt to

present Christianity to their peers, the cultured despisers not of real

religion but what they perceive religion to be. He followed up this initial

---

[24] Bosch, <u>Transforming Mission</u>, p. 450.

[25] William Warren Sweet, <u>The Story of Religion in America</u> (New York, NY: 1950), rev. ed., p. 2.

[26] Friedrich Schleiermacher, <u>Speeches on Religion to its Cultured Despisers</u> (NY: Harper, 1965).

work with <u>The Christian Faith</u>[27].

David Tracy calls Schleiermacher "the clerarest example—indeed, the still towering paradigm—for this liberal model."[28]

Thomas Jefferson was probably the most unabashedly theological of our presidents. He worked for many years to produce his appreciation of Jesus' teaching, from which he removed all the miracles, including Jesus' resurrection.[29] He called himself a deist and a Christian (logically, he could be one or the other, not both), and professed belief in the Christian heaven, something other deists did not. Martin Marty gives a positive evaluation of this liberal president. [30]

## American Liberal Protestantism, 1870's-1960's

After the Civil War, Protestantism optimistically confronted expansion and progress. Civility, tolerance, the vote for women, all were championed as positive values. Sweet noticed the link with science after World War I: "Those were the days when every branch of learning coveted some tie-up with the word science. It was indeed the charmed word." At the same time, the disintegration such an approach caused was also noted.[31] Newspaper columnist's Walter Lippmann's term "the

---

[27] Friedrich Schleiermacher, <u>The Christian Faith</u> (New York, NY: Harper, 1963), 2 vols., Introduction by Richard R. Niebuhr (pp. ix-xx).
[28] David Tracy, <u>Blessed Rage for Order</u> (Chicago, IL: University of Chicago Press, 1996), p. 26. See also Welch, <u>Protestant Christianity</u>, pp. 182-89.
[29] Thomas Jefferson, <u>Thomas Jefferson's Life of Jesus</u> (Springfield, IL: 1975).
[30] Martin E. Marty, "Preface," in <u>Jefferson and Religion</u>, Eugene R. Sheridan (Princeton, NJ: Princeton University Press, 1983), Thomas Jefferson Memorial Foundation, Monticello Monograph Series, 1998, pp. 7-9.
[31] William Warren Sweet, <u>Story of Religion in America</u>, p. 419.

acids of modernity" was later quoted by many observers, to describe the

corrosive effect of these factors on families, neighborhoods, etc.[32]

Between 1886 and 1926, the Student Volunteer Movement,

sometimes called "the World Council of Churches in short pants,"[33]

launched the modern American Protestant missionary movement. A

recent history is advertised as necessary "for better understanding one of

the greatest forces for modernity in this century [20th], the American

missionary movement."[34] Welch also observes: liberal theology, in some

of its forms, influenced the missionary movement, and was influenced by

it, especially in ecumenism.[35]

One of the most quoted experts on American Protestant liberalism,

Harvard Divinity School's William Hutchinson, notes that the liberals

began winning battles after the Civil War.

> . . . the milder liberal forces at work from within the
> churches enjoyed steady and rapid gains. Despite setbacks
> and heresy trials in most denominations, and a lack of any
> visible effect in some others, by the later nineteenth century
> Protestant liberalism was very much in the ascendant. The
> rise of fundamentalism, and of other highly defensive
> reactions, confirms rather then [sic] contradicts this
> judgement.[36]

---

[32] Martin Marty, "What Is Fundamentalism," Fundamentalism As an Ecumenical Challenge, (London: SCM Press, 1992, #3), Concilium, p. 11; Philip Gleason, Catholicism and Liberalism, p. 57, citing Lippmann's A Preface to Morals (NY: Macmillan, 1929).

[33] See Ruth Rouse and Stephen Charles Neill, A History of the Ecumenical Movement (Philadelphia, PA: Westminster, 1967), pp. 328-29; 601-12.

[34] Michael Parker, The Kingdom of Character: The Student Volunteer Movement for Foreign Missions, 1886-1926 (Lanham, MD: University Press of America, Inc., 1998), co-published with the American Society of Missiology.

[35] Welch, Protestant Christianity, pp. 211, 177-78, 290-301.

[36] William R. Hutchinson, ed., American Protestant Thought in the Liberal Era (Lanham, MD: University Press of America, 1984), p. 3.

Perhaps more importantly, Hutchinson claims that "by the 1920's they had made liberalism the acknowledged point of view in approximately half the Protestant theological seminaries."[37]  He also presents his reasoning that modernism came into vogue as a term and as a reality only in the last third of the nineteenth century.  He defines it as a special kind of liberalism, "the insistence that theology must adopt a sympathetic attitude toward secular culture and must consciously strive to come to terms with it."[38]

As we saw in ch. 3, the neo-orthodox criticism of liberal thought could be savage (above, p. 63).  Hutchinson believes that "Reinhold Niebuhr and his colleagues were unduly cataclysmic."  And he will show us below that "liberal theological ideas would straggle back from the neo-orthodox wars, but they would find the old homestead . . . altered almost beyond recognition."[39]

Yet the resurgence of Protestant liberalism in the 1950's and 1960's owed much to an appreciation of neo-orthodoxy, and a growing belief that "their neo-orthodox tormentors might themselves have represented a temporary adjustment within a continuing progressive movement."[40]  Hutchinson points out that the Confession of 1967, which focused Presbyterian and Reformed Churches' discussion of neo-orthodoxy, (ch. 3 above, pp. 61, 66) "at some points was a literal

---

[37] Ibid, pp. 4, 11.
[38] Ibid, p. 11.
[39] Ibid, p. 9.
[40] Ibid.

transcription of the ideas for which well-known liberals had contended in the 1870's."[41]  Among these are the deliberate silence on doctrines such as predestination, and the "most prominent and reiterated theme, next to the announced central one of divine-human reconciliation, . . .a recognition of the transience of humanly shaped creeds and institutions."[42]

Before we can examine the reemergence of Protestant liberalism in the 1990's, we must retreat to the Catholicism of the 1870's in the USA, and see why the repression of liberalism in American Catholicism made the events of Vatican II so explosive.  The convergence of Catholic and Protestant liberalism can only be appreciated through examining first the repression and then the bursting forth, especially in the USA of Vatican II.

## Americanism and Catholic Modernism (1880's – 1960)

In ch. 4, I sketched the fundamentalist side of the crisis in Catholicism knows as Americanism, and Catholic Modernism (p. 95). Vidler describes very well such varied European personalities as Father George Tyrrell, Baron Friedrich von Hugel, and Maude Petri.[43]  An especially tragic American figure was the leader of the Josephite community, Father John Slattery (1851-1926).  Founded with the

---

[41] Ibid, p. 226, printing the entire Confession through p. 233.
[42] Ibid, p. 226.
[43] Alec Vidler, A Variety of Catholic Modernists, (Cambridge:  Cambridge University Press, 1970).

Vatican's encouragement to minister to blacks in the United States, the American Josephites developed from the English Josephites of Mill Hill, London. Slattery was an early proponent of liberal ideas, which involved attacking "the American clergy and his fellow Irish Catholics for their racism." He eventually left the priesthood, married, abandoned Catholicism and practiced law.[44]

The doctoral thesis of R. Scott Appleby, who co-edited with Martin Marty the Fundamentalist Project described in ch. 4, is a marvelous description of Americanism, with an attempt to see how it anticipated Vatican II. Borrowing from William Hutchinson on Protestant liberalism, Appleby views modernism among Catholics in the USA as a special brand of liberalism, dating from 1870-1930, and differing "from other liberals by the level of self-awareness with which they appropriated the modern. . . . Modernists were fully aware that they were modernists."[45] In a remarkably sympathetic treatment, Appleby deals with the hopes of American Catholic progressives for meshing democratic values with their Catholic faith, with appreciating "liberties of thought, speech, and religion, and the rise of self-governing peoples."[46]

Unfortunately, Rome's fear that liberal and modernist efforts would lead to "the loss of the transcendent altogether" provoked a blanket

---

[44] William Murray, "Crusader, Visionary and Rebel," The Josephite Harvest, June 2001, pp. 4-5.
[45] R. Scott Appleby, "Church and Age Unite!" The Modernist Impulse in American Catholicism (Notre Dame, IN: University of Notre Dame Press, 1992), Notre Dame Studies in American Catholicism, pp. 1-2. Appleby documents the impact of the thorough attack on liberalism by Don Feliz Sarda y Salvany, Liberalism is Sin (St. Louis: Herder, 1899), as does Komonchak, in Catholicism and Liberalism, pp. 77 and 95, n. 1.
[46] Ibid, p. 238.

rejection of Catholic liberal and modernist efforts. [47] Appleby is especially good at sketching the "notable similarities" between the situation of the early 1900's, and Vatican II. He begins by noting that the theologians of today have "fellowship and a kind of protective cocoon" that Slattery and his companions did not have.[48] But the biggest similarity is that both invoked the "via media" of Cardinal John Henry Newman, who "anticipated and inspired much of the ground-breaking work of the modernists."[49]

As early as 1967, modernism expert Father John Joseph Heaney wrote that modernism "was characterized by a tone antagonistic to all ecclesiastical authority, and by a belief in an adaptation of the Church to what was considered sound in modern thought even at the expense of radically changing the Church's essence." [50] He then notes that modernists "fed on and assimilated many legitimate tendencies" such as development of dogmas, greater respect for Scriptural scholarship, a call to leave the cultural ghetto, etc.[51]

In 1994, the Jesuit think tank Woodstock Theological Center, and the Department of Government of Georgetown University published the results of their joint efforts (begun in the spring of 1989) to compare Catholicism and liberalism. Noting that formerly Catholicism and

---

[47] Ibid, p . 59.
[48] Ibid, p. 239.
[49] Ibid, pp. 240-41.
[50] J.J. Heaney, S.J., "Modernism," New Catholic Encyclopedia 9:995.
[51] Ibid.

liberalism had "stood in principled opposition," the authors observed "that both the teaching of the church and the premises of liberal thinking about our public life have changed significantly."[52]

A former editor of the liberal Catholic journal Commonweal, Peter Steinfels, contributed the analysis of the nineteenth century, calling it a time of "cycles of revival and rejection." His conclusion that "at all levels of the church, an interlocking system of surveillance, oaths, accusations and rebukes purges theological deviance" is probably accurate. Americanism, Christian Democracy, and modernism were all condemned by Pius X.[53] Then, as Steinfels notes, "Vatican II ultimately endorses most of the planks in the platform of nineteenth-century liberal Catholicism."[54] This volume, which I will call the Woodstock Project, demonstrates how Vatican II provided a new focus for viewing the past several centuries, especially since almost 30 years had elapsed between the end of the council in 1965 and the completion of the Woodstock Project in 1994.

One of the most intriguing observations in the project was made by Catholic historian Philip Gleason. He acknowledged that he was borrowing his key distinction from a very unique Catholic historian and diplomat who served as US ambassador to Spain during World War II,

---

[52] R. Bruce Douglass and David Hollenbach, S.J., Catholicism and Liberalism (Cambridge: Cambridge University Press, 1994), p. xv (underlining is italics in original).
[53] Peter Steinfels, "The failed encounter: The Catholic Church and Liberalism in the Nineteenth Century," Catholicism and Liberalism, pp. 20-21.
[54] Ibid, p. 21.

Carlton J.H. Hayes. In writing about liberals in late nineteenth century Europe, Hayes distinguished between "ecumenical" or "general" liberalism, and "sectarian liberalism." The former meant "the spirit animating developments from the Reformation through the French Revolution and its aftermath." Promoting the rights of the individual against the claims of traditional authority in church or state would include representative government and eliminating restrictions on commerce and industry. Christians could be liberal in this sense.[55]

However, "sectarian liberalism" took these elements and transformed them into "a doctrinaire ideology," professed mostly by agnostics and scientific materialists who were "not merely anti-clerical but rampantly anti-Christian." Gleason's adaptation of Hayes' distinction to the American scene is provocative.[56]

Gleason also shows how through the 1920's, there was some favorable interaction between the liberalism of the times and Catholic leaders, especially Mgr. John A. Ryan, "the most liberal of Catholic social theorists."[57] Nor was it any accident, as Gleason notes, that Commonweal was founded in 1924.[58]

But Fr. Charles Coughlin's attack on Roosevelt's New Deal (many Catholics favored the New Deal), the Spanish Civil War, and the

---

[55] Philip Gleason, "American Catholics and Liberalism, 1789-1960," Catholicism and Liberalism, p. 45; see 50-55 for Americanism.
[56] Gleason, Catholicism and Liberalism, pp. 45-47.
[57] Ibid, pp. 57, 61.
[58] Ibid, p. 58.

appointment of Myron C. Taylor as Roosevelt's personal representative to the Vatican all shifted fledging liberal Catholics away from their possible Protestant allies. It would not be until the 1960's that Catholic liberal tendencies would be active again.[59]

Gleason believes that John Courtney Murray's "ecumenical liberalism" attracted more and more Catholics of the "Commonweal liberalism" stripe.[60] This of course helped prepare the way for Vatican II's more open stance.

Stephen Krason also explains John Ryan's influence as "perhaps the preeminent example of an American Catholic figure earlier in this century who was involved actively with liberal efforts."[61] Krason not only lists the liberal organizations Ryan was active in, such as the American Civil Liberties Union, but makes an interesting case that Catholic immigrants were naturally attracted to political liberalism, concluding that "survey research indicates that this New Deal liberalism continued . . . through the 1950's."[62]

## Vatican II: A Liberal Council?

As we saw above in ch. 3, the 21st ecumenical council, Vatican II (1962-65) began with indications that it was not going to be the staid, "stamp what the Pope wants" meeting (pp. 65-66). But almost no one

---

[59] Ibid. pp. 61-64.
[60] Ibid, p. 67.
[61] Stephen M. Krason, Liberalism, Conservatism, and Catholicism (New Hope, KY: Catholics United for the Faith, Inc., 1991), p. 15.
[62] Krason, pp. 16-17.

expected that it would unleash the forces it did. Cardinal Avery Dulles evaluated it in 1990: "After several centuries of increasing centralization, Vatican Council II set the Catholic Church on a course of inner diversification."[63] To almost everyone's surprise, one of the streams which emerged is Catholic liberalism, or as its critics call it disparagingly, modernism.

Hollenbach, in the Woodstock Project, wrote "The Second Vatican Council marked the cessation of the battle of attrition fought between Catholics and liberals in the nineteenth and first half of the twentieth centuries."[64] Of course, this is a far less severe judgement of Vatican II than Wills and Hitchcock below. But it is most important, for it shows that the entire framework, between liberals and Christians with liberal sympathies has changed.

The sea change among Protestant youth, about 1960, away from neo-orthodoxy towards liberalism (see Introduction above, p. 1) occurred among Catholic youth with the opening of Vatican II in 1962. At least in the USA and whenever Irish families had emigrated, the election of John F. Kennedy in 1960 produced a tremendous burst of optimism. But it took several decades for those who took part in Vatican II, to notice the linkage. Cardinal Joseph Ratzinger, writing in 1982 saw "this fact: something of the Kennedy era pervaded the Council, something of the

---

[63] Cardinal Avery Dulles, S.J., "Catholicism and American Culture: The Uneasy Dialogue," America, Jan. 27, 1990, p. 54, originally a two part lecture at Fordham University, Dec. 5-6, 1989.
[64] Hollenbach, Catholicism and Liberalism, p. 323.

naïve optimism of the concept of the great society. We can do everything we want to do if only we employ the right means."[65]

Father Joseph Komonchak has a marvelous chapter in the Woodstock Project describing Vatican II's impact on liberalism. After detailing why Pope John XXIII criticized the "almost neurotic denial of all that was new,"[66] Komonchak concentrates on two documents, the Pastoral Constitution on the Church in the Modern World and the Declaration on Religious Freedom. He concludes that these two documents which look outside the Church, and the others which look at inner realities such as worship and Scripture, all "reflect a new and far more positive encounter with modernity," than did the attitude of Catholic leadership from 1900-62.[67]

Timothy McCarthy also singled out the Constitution of the Church in the Modern World as a basis for a "new humanism" which favors a developing Christian humanism, to avoid the excesses of secular humanism, while making common cause in certain areas.[68]

Even before Vatican II ended in 1965, liberal lay Catholics in the USA started their own weekly newspaper, the National Catholic Reporter, in 1964. Associated Press writer Maria Sudekum Fisher had no problem

---

[65] Joseph Ratzinger, Principles of Catholic Theology (San Francisco, CA: Ignatius Press, 1987) (German original, 1982), p. 372, referring also to a German work by Hans Kung..
[66] The words are Ratzinger's, describing the pope's attitude when the young Ratzinger wrote Theological Highlights of Vatican II (New York: Paulist Press, 1966), p. 23, cited by Komonchak, "Vatican II and the encounter between Catholicism and Liberalism,: Catholicism and Liberalism, p. 79.
[67] Komonchak, p. 80. (80-88).
[68] Timothy McCarthy, Christianity and Humanism (Chicago, IL: Loyola Press, 1996), pp. 47-48, citing Constitution on the Church in the Modern World, #'s 7, 55-56.

calling it "liberal" in her feature story of December, 2001. "Readership . .

. has held steady at about 50,000 for years."[69]

Komonchak's most valuable section is his analysis of the

"reception" of Vatican II. He attributes an important distinction to John

Courtney Murray:

> The broad liberal tradition he believed not only to be
> compatible with fundamental Catholic beliefs and values but
> in part to be inspired by them, and the doctrinaire liberalism
> whose exclusion of religion from public consequence he
> believed to be radically incompatible with Catholicism, both
> philosophically and theologically.[70]

If doctrinaire liberalism has replaced "the consensus which

underlay the original American experiment," then Christianity has no

room to dialogue with the cultured despisers of religion. But if religious

and moral principles, which are constitutive elements of the spiritual

substance of the American experiment, are still held by many, then the

dialogue must go on, and the documents of Vatican II furnish an opening

for such dialogue.[71] From antagonism and withdrawal, to working for a

public consensus which includes human rights adhering to persons

living in communities: this is the "epochal shift" represented by Vatican

II.[72]

However, as both Dulles and Komonchak noted, there are many

other voices within the post-Vatican II Catholic Church. From about

---

[69] Maria Sudekum Fisher, "National Catholic Reporter raises issues many in the church would like to keep private," Evening Sun (Norwich, NY), Dec. 28, 2001, p. 14.

[70] Komonchak, Catholicism and Liberalism, p. 89.

[71] Ibid, pp. 90-91.

[72] Ibid, pp. 90, 94.

1966-77, not only liberal, but radical tendencies pushed energetically for changes that left many puzzled at first, and then angry. During these years, the picture of the Catholic Church as a huge boulder, the largest of all denominations, emerged. It took a lot to get this boulder moving. But when it starts, as it did from 1966-77, many people and institutions in its way felt crushed by the changes.

Two of the most detailed and even harsh criticisms of these changes were published in the early 1970's. James Hitchcock, whom we met in ch. 4 (above, p. 114) addressed "the failure of the great hopes for reform which swept through the Church less than a decade ago."[73] He claimed to have been a "progressive" himself, and described the "liberal Catholic" of the 1950's.[74] While there are still "many progressives" who want "the limited and conservative reform" advocated before Vatican II, "the fulcrum of discussion has shifted sharply leftward in the past few years."[75] He then summarized the situation, which may be even more applicable after Sept. 11.

> Responsibility for the failure of aggiornamento must be about evenly apportioned between rigid reactionaries, especially in the hierarchy, who never believed in reform and did little to implement it, and radical innovators with little commitment to historic Catholicism who nonetheless had a disproportionate influence in the reform movement. Naturally, these two extremes have constantly fed on each other, each serving as a bogey which gives the other a

---

[73] James Hitchcock, The Decline and Fall of Radical Catholicism (New York, NY: Herder, 1971), p. 9.

[74] Hitchcock, Decline, pp. 9, 13-18.

[75] Ibid, p. 19.

certain credibility.[76]

The other 1971 critic, also a layman, Garry Wills, examined "doubt, prophecy and radical religion" following Vatican II. He explained how the liberalism of John F. Kennedy and Pope John XXIII worked together.[77] Wills presents the tragic situation of Catholic seminaries in the USA going through great crisis.[78] He also suggests that the Viet Nam War deeply influenced the liberal attitude, and indeed every attitude at this period.[79]

Two multi-volume assessments of Vatican II appeared with the minimum twenty-five year perspective, one in 1988, to mark twenty-five years since the beginning of the council in 1962, and one in 1995, giving it thirty years since the end of the council in 1965. Father Rene Latourelle's 1988 work is especially detailed on the atmosphere in the Catholic Church in the late 1950's and early 1960's, and the reversal of attitude towards theologians like Congar, Chenu, de Lubac, Danielou and particularly Teilhard de Chardin.[80]

Giuseppe Alberigo's 1995 work is excellent for his analysis of the strengths and weaknesses of Vatican II. "For Catholicism to live like a besieged fortress of truth was a condition of apparent strength and

---

[76] Ibid, p. 32.
[77] Garry Wills, Bare Ruined Choirs (Garden City, NY: Doubleday, 1971), pp. 79-96. See ch. 3 above, p. 65.
[78] Wills, Bare Ruined Choirs, pp. 214-29; Hitchcock, Decline, pp. 75-96.
[79] Wills, Bare Ruined Choirs, p. 56.
[80] Rene Latourelle, S.J., ed., Vatican II: Assessment and Perspective Mahwah, NJ: Paulist, 1988), especially Giacomo Martina, S.J., "The Historical Context in Which the Ideas of a New Ecumenical Council Was Born," pp. 30-40.

substantial weakness."[81]  As the council progressed, "people gradually become aware that those who were hoping for renewal still had only immature notions of what it involved."[82]

Alberigo's conclusion is the Pope John XXIII and Cardinal Bea pushed for a "trajectory" of openness and modernity, and the Vatican officials (the curia), for restraint, protectiveness and tradition.[83]

One hesitates to claim that Vatican II caused Catholic liberalism. When Reeves describes "the summer of 1968" as "the apex of the most revolutionary year of the century," he includes the assassinations of Martin Luther King Jr. and Robert Kennedy, riots in 125 cities, and could have added the increasingly polarizing Viet-Nam War and the political mess which would lead to the resignations of a vice-president and president.  Yet he does include the religious issue of the papal encyclical on birth control, Humanae Vitae, which led to a powerful liberal argument that the church should stay out of the bedroom.[84] Vatican II had opened a door for more democratic processes in the church, and the birth control encyclical indicated that the open door would be very hard to close.

---

[81] Giuseppe Alberigo, ed. History of Vatican II, Vol. I, Announcing and Preparing Vatican Council II, Toward a New Era in Catholicism (Maryknoll, NY:  Orbis, 1995), English version edited by Joseph A. Komonchak; "Conclusion:  Preparing For What Kind of Council," p. 504.
[82] Alberigo, Ibid, p. 505, crediting Cardinal Bea with repeatedly noting this.
[83] Ibid, pp. 506-08.
[84] Thomas C. Reeves, America's Bishop, p. 322.  He captures the impact of the encyclical on Bishop Fulton Sheen.

# 1965-2002:  Highlights of Protestant and Catholic Liberalism

Have Protestant and Catholic liberals increasingly reinforced each other?  As we examine the developments in both traditions, it would seem to be so.

When we look today at the books and films and TV series which enthralled people from the early 1960's through the 1970's, we are amazed at the way they attacked all institutions and tradition.  When we originally saw them, they seemed simply funny.  Today, to read J.D. Salinger's <u>Catcher in the Rye</u>,[85] to watch Charles Webb's movie <u>The Graduate</u>,[86] to view episodes of Norman Lear's <u>All in the Family</u>,[87] we are more disturbed at the way liberal media types manipulated us.  Catholics had come out of their ghetto; Catholic liberals increasingly were molded by the same influences as Protestant liberals.

Humor can have a leveling and uniting effect.  Both Catholic and Protestant liberals probably chuckle at a Larson cartoon which shows a boy covered with soot, standing at his shattered laboratory table.  Feathers are floating all over the room.  The caption reads:  "God, as a kid, tries to make a chicken in his room."[88]

Protestant and Catholic liberals both probably feel slightly

---

[85] J.D. Salinger, <u>Catcher in the Rye (Boston, MA:  Little, Brown, 1951).</u>
[86] Calder Willingham and Buck Henry, in 1967, adapted Webb's book (New York, NY:  New American Library, 1963).
[87] Jacqueline Cutler (Tribune Media Services), "A Tribute to Norman Lear," <u>Buffalo News</u>, TV topics, Aug. 25, 2002, pp. 24-25.
[88] Gary Larson, "The Far Side," March 21, 1992.

threatened by a Thaves "Frank and Ernest" cartoon showing Moses

checking out the Ten Commandments, He excitedly exclaims, "The

Libertarians are going to go bananas!"[89] (One of the jibes by

conservatives against liberals is that these are the Ten Commandments,

not the Ten Suggestions).

From Oct. 21-23, 1975 the national justice conference planned as

part of the U.S. Catholic Church's observance of the nation's

bicentennial took place in Detroit. Thirteen thousand forty delegates

acted as an advisory body to the U.S. bishops, approving resolutions in

eight areas, from the church through ethnicity and race. [90]

Cardinal Joseph Bernadin immediately saw the weakness of the

process as special interest groups had too much of a role.[91] Surprisingly,

Protestant liberals seem to have paid very little attention to the Detroit

meeting.[92]

Dulles notes that "the Detroit Call to Action conference sponsored

by the American bishops in 1976 was a triumph for liberal

Catholicism."[93] (He distinguishes between the liberalism of "many

leading scholars, such as the Rev. Richard P. McBrien, the Rev. Charles

E. Curran, Daniel Maguire and Jay Dolan," and radicalism of Dorothy

---

[89] Bob Thaves, "Frank and Ernest," March 5, 2002.
[90] See Origins, "Justice in the Church," Nov. 4, 1976, p. 309. This issue includes the resolutions in four areas.
[91] Joseph Bernadin, "Archbishop Sees Mixed Results," Origins, Nov. 4, 1976, p. 324.
[92] A search through Christian Century from Oct. 15 to Dec. 3 found not a single mention.
[93] Avery Dulles, S.J., "Catholicism and American Culture," America, Jan. 27, 1990, p. 56.

Day, Fathers Daniel Berrigan, S.J., and Matthew Fox, O.P.[94])

In 1998, Cardinal Francis George called liberal Catholicism "an exhausted project."[95] Its downward movement probably began as Catholic leaders examined the results of the Call to Action.

## Renewal at Two Parishes

The efforts of two Catholic parishes, one in Virginia during the early 1970's, and one in New York during the late 1990's, to implement Vatican II, may show what happened at the extreme left of liberal renewal attempts. Both were widely publicized.

Led by their pastor, Father Tom Quinlan. St. Mary's Church in Norfolk, VA took its case to Rome, which referred it back to the local bishop, Thomas Welsh (Arlington, VA diocese). Fr. Quinlan stayed in the priesthood. The parish council was dissolved by the new pastor.[96]

The Rochester, NY parish split and its pastor Father James Callan was first suspended, then excommunicated.[97] His movement, "Sprititus Christi," attempted to form communities in Buffalo and Syracuse.[98] Issues such as approving gay life style, and ordaining a woman co-pastor

---

[94] Ibid, p. 57. Fox has left the Catholic Church. Dulles short sketch of Catholic liberalism is very good: 56-59.

[95] See below, p. 239.

[96] Thomas Welsh, "A Parish in Conflict," Origins, Dec. 19, 1974, p. 412; Executive Committee of the Parish Council, "Dissent," ibid, p. 412-13, The National Catholic Reporter thoroughly covered the dispute.

[97] Associated Press, Buffalo News, Dec. 8, 1998, p. A-5; Ben Dobbin, AP Writer, Evening Sun (Norwich, NY), Feb. 25, 1999, p. 2.

[98] Council of Priests Minutes, Diocese of Buffalo, NY, March 21, 2000, p. 4, #5.

were cited the most often as liberal concerns carried too far.[99]

Note that in the 1970's case, few actually left Catholicism. In the 1990's one, many did. While one should not read too much into only two cases, these do seem more than symbolic. Positions have hardened over the two decades. For some, dialogue can only go so far.

## Secularism and Its Impact

One of the publishing sensations during 1965 was Harvey Cox's Secular City. Written merely as "a study resource for a series of conferences planned for 1965 by the National Student Christian Federation," the work unexpectedly captured the spirit of the time, perhaps at the high point of Protestant liberalism.[100] As a young professor of philosophical theology, I remember using his book with its very useful distinction between secularization (the process) and secularism (a philosophy which may exclude God). Just as useful was Claude Welch's responses in Secular City Debate that metaphysical questions about reality are always going to be posed and answers developed, even if Cox is right that no philosophical system will ever again be total and complete.[101]

Two authors brought important insights to the issue of liberal Christianity and secularism. Robert Wuthnow (an evangelical

---

[99] Dobbin, Evening Sun, Feb. 25, 1999, p. 2.

[100] Harvey Cox, Secular City (NY: Macmillan, 1965; rev. 1966), p. xi.

[101] Claude Welch, "Reflections on the Problem of Speaking of God," in Secular City Debate, ed. Daniel Callahan (NY: Macmillan, 1966), p. 163.

sociologist) in <u>The Struggle for America's Soul</u> (1989), examined how liberals and evangelicals have changed, perhaps because each was confronting secularism. Wuthnow concludes that "liberals have begun to recognize that a purely 'anything goes' attitude is neither as intellectually respectable nor as organizationally desirable as their parents might have thought."[102]

Stephen Carter, an African-American jurist, created a sensation in 1993, with <u>The Culture of Disbelief; How American Law and Politics Trivialize Religious Devotion</u>.[103] He sharpened this up with an article in <u>First Things</u> in 2002, "Liberalism's Religion Problem." Carter is deeply disturbed by the rejection of his employer, Yale University to accommodating a group of Orthodox Jewish students who objected to coed dormitories as promoting premarital sex. He concludes with a good description of the secular society of Western Europe and North America:

> The liberal state is uncomfortable with deep religious devotion—and, for the most part, so is its product, liberal law. Religious belief is reduced to precise parity with all other forms of belief, an act of leveling that is already threatening to religion itself. In practice, liberalism often reduces religion to an even smaller role than other belief systems, seeking to limit or shut off its access to the public square and often deriding the efforts of the religious to live the lives they think the Lord requires when those efforts seems to conflict with other liberal goals.[104]

Michaelsen notes "beginning in 1966, membership declines for

---

[102] Robert Wuthnow, <u>The Struggle for America's Soul: Evangelicals, Liberals & Secularism</u> (Grand Rapids, MI: Eerdmans, 1989), p. 175.
[103] Stephen L. Carter, <u>The Culture of Disbelief</u> (NY: BasicBooks, 1993).
[104] Stephen L. Carter, "Liberalism's Religion Problem," <u>First Things</u> March 2002 (#121), p. 22 (21-32).

many of the large ecumenical Protestant denominations became apparent. . . . Especially in the 1970s, the losses were staggering, with many of these bodies declining by 10 percent or more."[105]

Wuthnow is able to document this for "Presbyterianism, one of our flagship denominational traditions."[106] He examines the sociological reasons for the decline, and looks at it from the perspective of several levels: national, and congregational. He concluded: "The cleavage between liberal and conservative Presbyterians is, in my view, both serious and unfortunate."[107]

The United Church of Christ provides the best description of a denomination which is self described as liberal, and is paying the heaviest price. Barbara Zikmund has used her own UCC as "A Case Study," presenting the effort to include all points of view as ultimately becoming "so ponderous in its efforts to be inclusive that it ceased to function effectively," leaving "us tired and divided."[108]

An AP notice in April 2001, stated that "membership in the liberal denomination, currently 1,377,320, declined 14 percent during the decade."[109]

Michaelsen believes that liberal Protestantism became so weak

---

[105] Robert S. Michaelsen and Wade Clark Roof, Liberal Protestantism (New York, NY: Pilgrim Press, 1986), p. 7; statistics 1972-84: pp. 41-43.

[106] Wuthnow, The Struggle, p. 68.

[107] Ibid, p. 89.

[108] Barbara Zikmund, Liberal Protestantism, Robert S. Michaelsen, ed. (New York: Pilgrim Press, 1986), p. 191.

[109] AP notice, "In a decade, 327 Congregations Left the United Church of Christ," Evening Sun (Norwich, NY), April 20, 2001, p. 17.

that conservative Christians "now focused their fire not on liberal Protestantism, but on secular humanism." Liberals were pushed even more into the background, not only religiously but politically.[110]

Liberals tend to be sympathetic towards humanists and secularists. As an organized movement, humanism reached a new level in 1933, when Roy Wood Sellars, a "professor of philosophy at the University of Michigan, issued A Humanist Manifesto. . . . endorsed by thirty-four American intellectuals and educators," the most famous of whom was John Dewey (1859-1952).[111] Timothy McCarthy proceeds to explain the 1973 Humanist Manifesto II, and the 1980 A Secular Humanist Declaration.[112] He believes that "most Americans would probably subscribe to most of the ten statements" listed in the 1980 declaration, endorsing free inquiry, respect for reason, etc. But he concludes that "religious groups objected to three of their principles." Divine Guidance is eliminated in favor of human intelligence; scientific method is the most reliable way of understanding the world, and ethics is based solely on human experience.[113]

Secular humanists also tend to attack the Judaeo-Christian value system, sometimes even denying its existence. An editorial in the Fayetteville, NC Observer-Times, for example, snapped "The notion that

---

[110] Michaelsen, Liberal Protestantism, p. 9.
[111] Timothy G. McCarthy, Christianity and Humanism (Chicago, IL: Loyola University Press, 1996), p. 46.
[112] McCarthy, ibid, pp. 46-47.
[113] Ibid, p. 47.

there is such a thing as 'the' Judeo-Christian viewpoint is absurd."[114]

Three areas of American life in particular have been taken over by secularists: higher education, the media, and mental health care. Kenneth Lee, writing in the conservative American Enterprise Institute magazine, claimed that "conservative Republicans and Christian conservatives" are the victims of employment discrimination by many universities. He found these universities the most striking:

- Brown University – 54 on the left to 3 on the right.
- Cornell University – 166 to 6
- Harvard University – 50 to 2
- Stanford University 151 to 17
- University of California at San Diego – 99 to 6
- Syracuse University – 50 to 2

> A similar lopsided leftist imbalance [exists] at Penn State University, University of Maryland, Denver College, Pomona College, San Diego State University, University of Colorado at Boulder, State University of New York at Binghamton, and others including (of course) University of California at Berkeley.[115]

Surveys of the religion professed by leaders in the broadcast and print media show an overwhelming number of agnostics.[116] Contrast this with Joseph Califano's statement that "almost all our people profess a belief in God and 92 percent affiliate with a particular religion."[117] Califano, Secretary of Health, Education and Welfare from 1977-79, is currently president of the National Center on Addiction and Substance

---

[114] Editorial. "Those Books Again," Fayetteville (NC) Observer-Times, Nov. 22. 1992, p. 2G.

[115] Cited by Wes Vernon, NewsMax.com Washington Editor, Sept. 5, 2002, p. 1.

[116] See for example Richard Lowry, "The High Priests of Journalism," American Family Association Journal, August, 1999, pp. 4-5.

[117] Joseph a. Califano, Jr., "Religion, Science and Substance Abuse," America, Feb. 11, 2002, p. 9.

Abuse, Columbia University, and was writing to bring together priests and psychiatrists, to combat substance abuse. He claims "only 40 percent to 45 percent of mental health practitioners believe in God." Even less see any role for religion in mental health.[118]

On the one hand, liberal Christians are able to speak the same language and frequent the same circles as militant secularists in higher education, the media and mental health. On the other hand, one gets the impression that frequently they fail to boldly challenge these leaders.

In 1986, the appearance of feminist theologian Rosemary Radford Ruether, a self-described "Catholic of liberal-left convictions," in America marked a new stage for that journal's relations with liberals.[119] Before Ruether wrote her manifesto, America had been most reluctant to have its writers describe themselves as liberals. The volume of letters to the editor showed that Ruether's challenge "to take seriously our responsibility, as liberal-left lay Catholics, for the future of the institutional church" was noted both by her supporters and opponents.[120]

---

[118] Ibid, p. 10.

[119] Rosemary Radford Ruether, "Crises and Challenges of Catholicism Today," America, March 1, 1986, p. 152.

[120] Ibid; "Letters," April 19, 1986 (America printed a "sampling," the first letter, one from Wallace Alcorn, a conservative Protestant minister), pp. 330-32.

# 1992, Fifth Centenary, National and World Council of Churches

When Hispanic Catholics took the lead in celebrating the 500 years of Columbus' arrival, liberal Protestants found out how much they misunderstood this segment of Catholicism. In 1990, the National Council of Churches Governing Board condemned the anniversary, noting that Columbus' arrival brought "invasion, genocide, slavery, 'ecocide' and the exploitation of the wealth of the land."[121]

This, described as "mindlessness masked as progress," by Father Allan Figueroa Deck, S.J., a leading Hispanic Catholic theologian, was not the most unkind cut; Deck documented the Catholic effort itself to celebrate the fifth centenary, as "a sorry chapter," led by "the so called progressives, the liberals." Rather than being "on the cutting edge," they "were simply out to lunch."[122]

Today, both the National Council of Churches, and the World Council of Churches, are accurately described as dominated by liberal Christianity. (Both groups do make efforts to include at least some of the other four viewpoints, especially catholic and evangelical/charismatic.) Gunter Gassmann, director of the WCC's Commission on Faith and Order from 1984-94, wrote frankly that the World Council "is clearly dominated and shaped by a liberal Protestant ethos in its organizational procedures, programmes, attitudes toward forms of worship, and in

---

[121] Cited by Thomas Reeves, <u>The Empty Church: The Suicide of Liberal Christianity</u>, p. 163.
[122] Allan Figueroa Deck, "The Trashing of the Fifth Centenary," <u>America</u>, Dec. 19, 1992, p. 499.

many of its theological perspectives."[123]

Both the Catholic hierarchy, and especially liberal Protestants, have great difficulty in dealing with immigrant groups, particularly the first generation. As Will Herberg showed in his classic work, though, by the third generation the situation has changed.[124]

## Pope John Paul II's Personalism, Especially Regarding the Death Penalty

One of the unexpected developments of the 1980's and 1990's was John Paul II's personalism. He called this concern for human dignity "the work of divine providence":

> If we consider the history of the last two centuries, we realize how people have become more aware of the value of the human person, of the rights of men and women, a universal longing for peace, a desire to do away with borders and racial divisions, a tendency for peoples and cultures to meet, tolerance towards those who are different, commitment to solidarity and voluntary work, rejection of political authoritarianism and the consolidation of democracy and an aspiration to more balanced international justice in the economic field.[125]

The most startling, for many Catholics and Protestants, is the pope's increasing skepticism of the death penalty. Avery Dulles, in his Laurence McGinley Lecture of Oct. 17, 2000, spends 90 percent of the

---

[123] Gunther Gassmann, "Fifty Years WWC-Gratitude and Uncertainty," Ecumenical Trends 27 (Dec. 1998, #11): 2/161. The entire article (1/160 4/163) is worthwhile. For NCC, see Reeves, Empty Church, pp. 161-65.

[124] Will Herberg, Protestant-Catholic-Jew, rev. ed. (Garden City, NY: Doubleday, 1960).

[125] John Paul II, "A Message for World Mission Sunday," Oct. 18, 1998 (New York, NY: Society for the Propagation of the Faith, 1998), p. 5.

lecture explaining how the use of Scripture and tradition has almost unanimously supported the death penalty until 1950. He then observes "in our day, a new recognition of the dignity and inalienable rights of the human person has dawned."[126] He concludes:

> The pope and the bishops, using their prudential judgement, have concluded that in contemporary society, at least in countries like our own, the death penalty ought not to be invoked, because, on balance, it does more harm than good. I personally support this position.[127]

## 1998-99: Commonweal, Cardinal George and Liberal Christianity

Soon to be Cardinal Francis George delivered a sermon on Jan. 17, 1998, at Chicago's Old St. Patrick's Church. In a "semi-famous moment," he said: "liberal Catholicism is an exhausted project."[128] This led one of the listeners, Commonweal's editor Margaret Steinfels, to invite him to elaborate, which produced the most recent thorough analysis of the strengths and weaknesses of liberal Christianity, the forum "The Crisis of Liberal Catholicism," at Loyola University, Chicago, on October 6, 1999.[129]

Cardinal George's presentation did also critique "a type of conservative Catholicism, which makes the same error as liberals in an

---

[126] Avery Dulles, S.J., The Death Penalty: A Right to Life Issue, (New York, Fordham University, 2000), p. 9.

[127] Ibid, p. 18. This is one of the few McGinley lectures not printed in America: for a copy, write Laurence J. McGinley Chair, Rose Hill Campus, 441 East Fordham Road, Bronx, NY 10458.

[128] Margaret O'Brien Steinfels, "Introduction," Commonweal, Nov. 19, 1999, p. 23.

[129] Describing "liberal Catholicism" as being "a central one" of some of Commonweal's "founding ideas," Steinfels published the two presentations and the three respondents in the Nov. 19, 1999 issue, pp. 24-45.

excessive preoccupation with the Church's visible government."[130]  He did acknowledge a debt to early liberals, such as Cardinal Newman, "in restoring to the center of the Church's consciousness the Gospel's assertion that Christ set us free," and enabling "the Church herself to break free of the conservative societal structures in which she had become imprisoned."[131]  However, George noted that:

> Personal experience becomes the criterion for deciding whether or not Jesus is my savior, a point where liberal Catholics and conservative Protestants seem to come to agreement, even if they disagree on what salvation means. Liberal culture discovers victims more easily than it recognizes sinners, and victims don't need a savior as much as they need to claim their rights.[132]

Perhaps the most thought-provoking response was given by the influential Washington Post columnist E.J. Dionne.  He elaborated on the liberalism of Pope John Paul II, claiming that the pope's decision to "confirm" dialogue with modernity, rather than reject it, pushed liberal Catholicism to the fore.  Dionne calls for "critical engagement" with the modern world, rather than confrontation or capitulation.  He concluded: "liberal Catholicism is providing answers that many people are looking for."[133]

---

[130] Francis George, O.M.I., "The Crisis of Liberal Catholicism," Commonweal, Nov. 19, 1999, p. 26.

[131] Ibid, p. 28.

[132] Ibid.

[133] E.J. Dionne, Jr., "We're All Liberals Now, Even the Pope," Commonweal, Nov. 19, 1999, pp. 44-45.

# Liberal Worship

James H. Nichols called our attention to the role of liberals in making worship clear and intelligible (above, p. 131). Vatican II began with worship renewal, because of the perceived need to simplify it. But liberalism tends to go too far; it has a built-in problem with public worship. One of the anecdotes of the 1960's concerns the Protestant pastor who was tired of seeing his congregation routinely and thoughtlessly bow their heads every Sunday as he intoned the formula "Let us bow our heads and pray." One Sunday, he deliberately and loudly replaced the standard formula with: "Lift up your heads, you SOB's; God made you good." The story admits he got their attention, but does not conclude how long he stayed as pastor.[134]

The ecumenical worship of the General Assemblies of the World Council of Churches has sought to be relevant, especially in 1991 in Canberra, Australia. It provoked much reaction from the Eastern Orthodox Churches, and led to more thought-out guidelines for worship involving our different streams.[135]

Public worship, or liturgy needs to combine tradition, with intelligibility. Moderate liberals remind us of this; radical liberals sometimes destroy what they are attempting to do in public worship. A

---

[134] A search for the source of this story has been fruitless.

[135] "News," Ecumenical Trends 20 (March 1991, #3) 35-36. John Erickson is very good on the overall picture, especially the blurring between "mainstream 'canonical' Orthodoxy and 'traditionalist' Orthodoxy": "A Retreat from Ecumenism," Ecumenical Trends 30 (Oct. 2001, #9): 8/136-9/137.

"reverent liberal" is almost a contradiction in terms.

## Are Liberals Closed?

One of the most damaging accusations to make to a liberal Christian is that they are as closed as the fundamentalists they oppose. C.S. Lewis talked to a group of English air force personnel; one of his listeners recorded what has become a standard observation.

> Lewis told us what it had cost him, as an Oxford don, to be a Christian. One might have expected to find within a university environment, and particularly at Oxford University, that home of lost causes, some measure of tolerance and liberality, some recognition and acceptance of the sanctity of honest belief and sincere conviction. Lewis discovered, as others have discovered before and since, that in this world there are few persons so illiberal as those who claim to be rational. His liberal and rational friends, he explained, did not object to his intellectual interest in Christianity; it was, they agreed, a proper subject for academic argument and debate; but to insist on seriously practicing it—that was going too far. He did not mind being accused of religious mania, that familiar gibe of the natural man; what he was unprepared for was the intense hostility and animosity of his professional colleagues.[136]

More recently, Ronald Rolheiser has noted the same tendency in contemporary liberals. After mentioning "the underappreciation that we liberals in general have had for movements" from Promisekeepers through the Charismatics to Alpha, he concludes "offended in our liberal sensitivities, we become fundamentalist ourselves—uncompromising,

---

[136] Stuart Barton Babbage, "To the Royal Airforce," <u>C.S. Lewis, Speaker and Teacher</u>, Caroline Keefe, ed., pp. 100 ff.

unnuanced, locked into a pre-prescribed view."[137]

## Conclusion

One of the more intriguing icons of the 1960's was Joseph Heller's violent anti-World War II satire Catch-22.[138] Now reading TV anchorman Tom Brokaw's The Greatest Generation,[139] one cannot believe that both men are viewing the same war. It may be hard to swallow, but perhaps both are viewing the same reality from different perspectives, and each is needed to get the total picture.

Each year, Columbus Day (the second Monday in October) reminds us of the Catholic origins of the USA. Less than six weeks later each year, Thanksgiving Day reminds us of the Pilgrim Protestant origins. Liberal Protestants, and even the Catholic hierarchy, fumbled the ball for the 1992 Fifth Centenary of Columbus's arrival. After Vatican II, Catholics developed a greater appreciation of what the pilgrim origins of this country meant, with a special Mass for that celebration. Can liberal Protestants and Catholics meet and challenge our culture, especially as these holidays are observed?

When Hollenbach concluded the Woodstock Project, he observed that the battle between Catholics and liberals ended with Vatican II (above, p. 142), and he concluded: the commitment of Catholicism to

---

[137] Ron Rolheiser, O.M.I., "Three Things for Liberals to Ponder," Catholic Northwest Progress, Aug. 1, 2002, p. 12.

[138] Joseph Heller, Catch 22 (NY: Simon & Schuster, 1961).

[139] Tom Brokaw, Greatest Generation (NY: Random House , 1998).

democracy and human rights "can be expected to be irrevocable."[140] While admitting that the Catholic Church "has much to learn from its liberal interlocutors,"[141] Hollenbach offers three areas where Catholicism (and especially its liberal adherents) can further the dialogue: emphasis on community, the value of civil conversation, and the importance of self-transcendence for "both freedom and genuine community among persons."[142]

Wuthnow, in his very challenging epilogue, raises the possibility that the more militant conservative religion becomes, the more militant liberal religion becomes, and vice versa. Both would be weaker were it not for the other. He asks liberals to "in fact provide an alternative to fundamentalism." And he asks evangelicals to "present themselves as an alternative to religious liberalism."[143]

---

[140] David Hollenbach, S.J., <u>Catholicism and Liberalism</u>, p. 323.
[141] Ibid, p. 337.
[142] Ibid, pp. 324-25.
[143] Wuthnow, <u>Struggle for America's Soul</u>, pp. 182-83.

# Conclusion and Beginning

> Charity means pardoning what is unpardonable, or it is
> no virtue at all.  Hope means hoping when things are
> hopeless, or it is no virtue at all. . . .  As long as matters are
> really hopeful, hope is a mere flattery or platitude; it is only
> when everything is hopeless that hope begins to be a
> strength.
>
>                                      Gilbert Chesterton[1]

Reese could write in 1996 about "the 'seven sisters' of American

Protestantism:  The American Baptist Churches in the USA, the

Christian Church (Disciples of Christ), the Episcopal Church, the

Evangelical Lutheran Church in America, the Presbyterian Church

(USA), the United Church of Christ, and the United Methodist Church."[2]

Fifty years ago, the situation was much different.  Few would have

included the Lutherans (they were too Germanic and Scandinavian).  The

Presbyterians were still split into two large denominations and several

smaller.  The United Church of Christ did not exist until 1957, when the

Congregational Churches and the Evangelical and Reformed Church

merged.  The last fifty years represent, on the one hand, a great leveling

of Protestantism, with the above Churches now viewed as tending

towards liberalism.  (CUIC has made an impact, especially concerning

Afro-American issues, on most of these Churches).

On the other hand, the Missouri Lutheran Synod reminds us that

fundamentalism and even catholicism dominate this Church.  As we

---

[1] Cited by Garry Wills, <u>Bare Ruined Choirs</u>, p. 251.

[2] Thomas C. Reeves, <u>The Empty Church</u>, p. 1, admitting that not all agree with his analysis (n. 1).

ended the 20th century, voices within Catholicism, such as Greeley and Ratzinger emphasized that many were disillusioned with the results of Vatican II reform. History has repeated itself: James Hastings Nichols wrote that it is "sobering" to inquire as to why the Reformation of the 16th century "had such qualified success." He then observed in 1968, after participating in Vatican Council II:

> Even the best of liturgical scholarship, pastoral concern, theological power may not suffice today. All the resources of Protestantism and Roman Catholicism together will be strained to interpret and convey Biblical realities to the modern masses, dominated by the mentality of a technological industrialized age.[3]

The fundamentalist-liberal split seems to be worsening. Reformed Vatican II Christians do not have the leadership which they enjoyed when Karl Barth and Karl Rahner were alive. Catholics, especially in the Roman Catholic Church, have lost prestige since the pedophilia crisis. Does this mean that the evangelical/charismatic way is the future?

On June 20, 2002, an American Oblate priest who has been a missionary in Brazil for 40 years came to dinner at our rectory in Buffalo, NY. He described attending a planning session of the Alpha Program, at the Catholic Church in the Buffalo diocese where he was staying. He remarked that he was very struck by the way the Alpha Program (ch. 2 above, p. 41) places first and foremost the relationship of each person with Jesus Christ. He reminded me that the tendency in the catholic

---

[3] James Hastings Nichols, <u>Corporate Worship</u>, p. 169; see also Wills, <u>Bare Ruined Choirs</u>, pp. 260-65.

way is to neglect that relationship and concentrate on the Church, the community.

The following Sunday, June 30, I was visiting my brother in Albuquerque, NM, and we attended Mass at Sacred Heart Church, a bilingual parish in the heart of the Hispanic section. We did not realize that this is the parish where Fr. Richard Rohr, O.F.M., one of the most influential charismatic priests, is in residence.[4] Fr. Rohr celebrated the noon Mass, in English, in a very moderate charismatic style. What deeply impressed me was the number of men in the congregation: men who served as Eucharistic ministers, ushers, etc. And the number of young families, with husbands and fathers, was very noticeable.

Protestant historians have continuously noted a small but important group of Christians: evangelical liberals.[5] Conservative in belief and liberal in justice matters, these Christians seem to be a growing number, especially in the charismatic movement. Probably the fact that both evangelical/charismatics and liberals insist on the dignity of the human person gives them both a basis for active involvement in bringing more equity to matters economic and governmental. Acute observers of the papacy have noted that, since the administration of Leo XIII, popes have tended to be conservative in belief and liberal in matters

---

[4] See Richard Rohr, O.F.M., with John Bookser Feister, Hope Against Darkness (Cincinnati, OH: St. Anthony Messenger Press, 2002), among his many books; among his audiocassettes, New Great Themes of Scripture (Cincinnati, OH: St. Anthony Messenger Press, 2002.

[5] For example, Winthrop Hudson, Religion in America, pp. 269-74; Princeton Seminary's Donald Macleod, Word and Sacrament (Englewood Cliffs, NY: Prentice-Hall, 1960), and especially "Worship and Evangelism," Princeton Seminary Bulletin 50 (May, 1957): 26.

of social justice.  This may account for John Paul II's concern about the death penalty.

In 1993, I wrote in the charismatic journal <u>New Covenant</u> that charismatics and liberals shared this concern for the dignity of the individual, which could be a source of convergence and joint action.[6] Then I waited for either rejection or enthusiastic approval.  Neither happened.  To me, this indicates that reality is there, waiting and developing quietly; journals such as <u>Sojourners</u> also demonstrate it.[7]

The annual meetings of the American Society of Missiology have brought people sympathetic to all five ways together since 1972.  One of its members, Frederick W. Norris, of Milligan College, TN described himself as "a conservative Protestant, probably an Evangelical, although I thought of myself as a free-church catholic."  Norris neatly summarized the evolution which many have gone through.[8]

Recently, a much younger group began, explicitly joining strict adherence to one's Church with a great concern for Christian unity (ecumenism).  Now ten years old, the Regeneration Forum demonstrates that Christians "who are seriously different from themselves" can converse and interact with each other.  Three related initiatives achieve this:  the magazine re:  generation quarterly (sic), local RQ Forums, and

---

[6] Harry E. Winter, O.M.I., "Charismatics Can Be Bridge Builders, <u>New Covenant</u>, May, 1993, p. 9.

[7] Jim Wallis, Editor-in Chief, <u>Sojourners</u> (six issues a year):  PO Box 2056, Marion, OH 43306; 1-800-678-9691;

[8] Frederick W. Norris, <u>The Apostolic Faith:  Protestants and Roman Catholics</u> (Collegeville, MN: Liturgical Press, 1992), the bibliography is excellent, and notes:  see pp. 156-59 for his cautious optimism that conservative Protestants and Catholics can work together.

the annual gathering The Vine.[9]

Another meeting place, this one joining the catholic imagination, liberal education, and the arts, is the Center for Religious Humanism (Seattle Pacific University, Methodist)'s journal of the arts and religion Image. Begun in 1989, Image features contributors such as Robert Coles, Annie Dillard, Elie Wiesel and Madeleine L'Engle. Annual conferences and summer workshops bring religious people together, on the cutting edge of the arts.[10]

During the 1970's the slogan became popular in religious education circles: Religion is caught, not taught.[11] Representing a reaction to memorization of texts as the heart of religious training, the slogan made neo-orthodox and Vatican II leaders very uneasy, for it violated the "both-and" principle so dear to them. Religion is both caught and taught, with the first being more critical, but the second important.

Bishop Edward Braxton's appreciation praising Karl Rahner shows the nostalgia for the giants of Vatican II,[12] and the lack of strong voices within Catholicism attempting to hold together two almost contradictory principles. The leader most articulate is perhaps Cardinal Walter Kasper, president of the Pontifical Council for Promoting Christian

---

[9] Tim Drake, "The 'Re-' Generation?" National Catholic Register, Oct. 13-19, 2002, p. 17: www.regenerator.com.
[10] www.imagejournal.org, Bo Caldwell, "Between God and Me: Five Days on a Silent Retreat," Image 19 (Spring, 1998): it was condensed in Catholic Digest, Dec. 1998, pp. 59-65.
[11] The author of this quote has not been found.
[12] Edward Braxton, "Letters to the Editor," America, Oct. 30, 1999, pp. 29-30.

Unity.[13]

There is no doubt that the catholic stream is growing steadily. Colleen Carroll, a reporter for the St. Louis Post-Dispatch, recently documented this.[14] John Kavanaugh, one of Carroll's professors in the doctoral program in the philosophy department of the University of St. Louis, listed "institutions of higher learning throughout the country," where there is a veritable "eruption" of faculty and students seeking a reasoned and prayerful orthodoxy.[15] On the other hand, a "young progressive" Catholic, Tom Beaudoin, severely criticized Carroll.[16]

In 1962, novelist J.F. Powers commented that American Catholic seminaries were "now thoroughly Americanized and turning out policemen, disc jockeys, and an occasional desert father."[17] Recently, James J. Gill commented on the allegation that some of those seminaries today are engaged in a bitter battle between orthodox and liberal seminarians.[18] While he disagreed with investigative reporter Michael S. Rose, he does worry about what happens when young priests from

---

[13] See Philip Blosser, "The Kasper-Ratzinger Debate & The State of the Church." New Oxford Review, 69 (April 2002, #4) 18-25; Kilian McDonnell, O.S.B., "Walter Kasper On Being a Bishop of a Local Church in a Universal Church?." Ecumenical Trends 31 (Dec. 2002, 11) 7/167-11/171.

[14] Colleen Carroll, The New Faithful: Why Young Adults Are Embracing Christian Orthodoxy (Chicago, IL: Loyola University Press, 2002); interview by Kathryn Jean Lopez, "The Believer Generation," National Catholic Register, Sept. 1-7, 2002, pp. 1, 10; Sept. 8-14, 2002, p. 16, claiming the same tendency in Judaism and Islam. Her book is a Sept. 2002 selection by Liguori Press's Theological Book Service: www.theobooks.org.

[15] John F. Kavanaugh, S.J., "Practicing the Faith," America, Nov. 4, 2002, p. 19.

[16] Tom Beaudoin, "In Need of Absolutes," review of The New Faithful, America, Nov. 11, 2002, pp. 35-37.

[17] J.F. Powers, Morte D'Urban (Garden City, NY: Doubleday, 1962), p. 177.

[18] James J. Gill, S.J., M.D., "Seminaries Await Vatican Visitation," America, July 15-22, 2002, pp. 10-13.

different sides have to live and work together.[19]

We may not have wanted to; we may not ultimately be responsible for it, but we are giving our young Christians a world unlike any we have ever known. The five ways of being Christian can seriously divide and hinder our witness, or some means and places may be found where these ways strengthen each of us.

Teams have been formed of two to three people, so that each team is sympathetic and knowledgeable in all five ways. These teams are available to work with bishops and other middle judicatory leaders, groups of pastors of large parishes and congregations, clusters of small ones, convocations of diocesan clergy, leaders of religious orders, etc. Use web site Five Ways Fellowship for the latest information.[20]

Do we have historical precedents for all five groups existing at the same time? It would have to be a time of peace, especially for the liberals and catholics. The age of Constantine, in the fourth and fifth centuries; the Renaissance—these are the only two possibilities. What is certain is that all five have never existed together as they have since 1950-2000, in the English speaking world.

As we go to press, two Jesuit priests engaged in a fascinating discussion in America over the interpretation of Vatican II. Avery Dulles and John W. O'Malley differed charitably but firmly. Dulles continues to

---

[19] Michael S. Rose, Goodbye: Good Men (Washington, DC: Regnery, 2002).
[20] The Five Ways Fellowship web site, http://www.buffomi.org/fiveways.htm, is administered from St. Rose of Lima Catholic Church, Buffalo, NY.

resist liberal interpretations; O'Malley insists that such are not foreign to the spirit or "style" of Vatican II.[21]

Evangelical Wheaton College announced that conservative Catholics William F. Buckley, Jr., and Adam Schwartz, (Christendom College), would be among the speakers at its May 22-23, 2003 "Malcolm Muggeridge Centenary" observance. The publicity noted that Wheaton's Marion E. Wade Center is collecting "all materials by and about seven notable British Christian authors: Owen Barfield, G.K. Chesterton, C.S. Lewis, George MacDonald, Dorothy L. Sayers, J.R.R. Tolkien and Charles Williams." Among the three co-sponsors is <u>Image: A Journal of the Arts & Religion</u> (see Center for Religious Humanism, above).[22]

May this book help Christians of all five ways see that to bring the Gospel message to our troubled and challenging times, we first have to name the problem and analyze it accurately. It is my hope and prayer that you have found this book a step in the right direction.

---

[21] Avery Dulles, S.J., "Vatican II: The Myth and the Reality," <u>America</u>, Feb. 24, 2003, pp. 7-11; John O'Malley, S.J., "The Style of Vatican II," pp. 12-15. Both John F. Long, S.J. and Francis A. Sullivan, S.J. seemed to side with O'Malley: "Further Reflections," March 17, 2003, pp. 14-15. Dulles and O'Malley continued their discussion in the March 31 issue, pp. 11-17.

[22] Conference registration online at <u>www.muggeridge.org</u>

APPENDIX: RONALD REAGAN'S INDUCTION SPEECH INTO THE FRENCH ACADEMY: "IF I HAD KNOWN VON BALTHASAR."

Note: President Reagan became the sixth of our presidents to be inducted into the French Academy (June 15, 1989). This fact went almost unnoticed in both the religious and secular press of the USA; the text of his speech, a eulogy on his predecessor, Cardinal Hans Urs von Balthasar, completely unreported. The following is taken from the review 30 Days, (July-Aug, 1989, pp. 41-42), published in Europe. I believe it is an interesting combination of catholic and liberal themes, from a president viewed as conservative.

I did not come to talk about my entering but another's passing. On June 26 of last year, my predecessor in this academy, the Swiss theologian Hans Urs von Balthasar died, two days before he was to become a cardinal. God called Father von Balthasar to a more eternal and exalted position.

Someone once remarked that if German theologians saw two doors, one marked "Heaven" and the other marked "Discussion on Heaven," they would go in the second. There is no doubt in my mind which one the Swiss father would enter. He loved knowledge because it led to the Lord.

It is the tradition of this Institut that the incoming member speak of the departed member. This I am very pleased to do, because I revere what I have come to know Father von Balthasar represented. He was a man of thought and reflection in a world of movement and activity. His mind ranged across the cosmos of God, across the ages of man, across the breadth of the human heart. He was a man of astonishing intellect and faith, so it is not surprising he was called the greatest theologian of this century; for what is theology other than the intellect of faith?

I do not think it is an embarrassment to be honest. I did not previously know of Father von Balthasar. Before I began working on these remarks, I did not know his works, which are of enormous proportions, filling scores and scores of volumes. Much of his writing is complex. He assumed his reader was as gifted and knowledgeable as he. He did not flaunt his intellect; it was just that his mind was more complete than most.

Father von Balthasar and I came from different worlds. We pursued different paths in life. At the peak of his life, he contemplated and quietly wrote of God, man, the radiance of the Church, the splendor of the truth that flows from Jesus Christ, and the revelations of faith, beauty and culture. At the peak of my life, I was surrounded by the noise of crowds and helicopters, by the push of television cameramen, and by the jangle of modern political realities. His world was the eternal one of the mind and spirit. Mine was current and secular. He saw the world cosmically. I saw the world by its daily crises. Yet we both had a certain vision for man and what he could be. And, yes, we both prayed to God so that we might better understand how we humans ought to live in this world. I learned the truth of a statement by Abe Lincoln when he was president. He said, "I could not perform the duties for one hour if I did not know that I could call upon One who was stronger and wiser than all others."

If some evening we had been able to share a cognac, our chairs pulled together in front of a fire somewhere, I think we could have found a common ground for understanding and appreciating each other's worlds.

I would have sought to draw upon his knowledge of the ages. Cardinal Henri de Lubac said of him, "The light from so many ancient sources allows him to illuminate the present . . ." I would have liked to ask Father von Balthasar, with his perspective of the centuries, about the political dilemmas of our times.

I would have liked to talk to him about those areas we held in common – like our common belief in the dignity of man and man's God-given right to pursue his own mission in life. Father von Balthasar represented the freedom of thought and faith that every individual on our earth deserves by birth. He was a man of thought who could not have survived in a totalitarian society, except in exile or prison. He would not have bowed to any obedience but God's. He would not have allowed his mind to be chained, and, in fact, no chains would have been strong enough to hold his intellect.

Father von Balthasar symbolized truth and knowledge and faith. Ladies and gentlemen, I am more optimistic than I ever have been in my life that the values he represented are ascendant in the world. And the reason is because of something that was foreign to him. Technology. In the modern age the word can reach farther, faster, to more people more easily than ever before. The technology is dazzling. Did you know that we have the ability, right now, to transmit the entire contents of the Encyclopedia Britannica in a one second burst of light? Did you know that we can store all the books in our Library of Congress in a computer no larger than a newspaper kiosk? And we can send this information from anywhere to anywhere. All this technology has breathtaking consequences for freedom and knowledge.

I believe that more than armies, more than diplomacy, more than the best intentions of democratic nations, the communications revolution will be the greatest force for the advancement of human freedom the world has ever seen. And to use the title of Father von Balthasar's trilogy, this development will work to The Glory of the Lord.

All of us here have seen the spirit of democracy loose upon the earth in recent months. The communications revolution is helping to get that spirit free and to spread its message. Amazing things are afoot in the world this spring.

In China . . . from a building opposite the Great Wall of the People hung a banner with one word on it – democracy. At the barricades, students and workers flashed the sign that has become the symbol of the Chinese democratic movement – the V for Victory. The Chinese government hasn't learned something very elemental that Father von Balthasar knew by instinct and reason – you cannot massacre an idea. You cannot run tanks over hope. You cannot riddle a people's yearning with bullets. Ladies and gentlemen, those heroic Chinese students who gave their lives have released the spirit of democracy and it cannot be called back.

That spirit is loose upon the world this spring. In Hungary, the government has begun dismantling part of the electrified barbed wire fence along the border with Austria. The country is moving toward a democratic, multiparty system. It increasingly looks like the question is not if, but when. As one man said, Hungary is a nation that is "beginning to forget its fear."

In Poland, the Polish Parliament has enacted a landmark law legalizing the Roman Catholic Church for the first time under communist rule. It's restoring the property and privileges stripped from the Church following World War II. Just last week, millions of Poles turned out in the most democratic election in more than four decades to repudiate the years of repression.

In the Soviet Union, the great dissident and our fellow member, Andrei Sakharov, is elected to the Congress of Peoples' Deputies. The peoples of the Baltic States press for their national identity in open, even defiant, ways. *Glasnost* is releasing forces of free thought that are time bombs for Soviet communism if it does not continue to change and liberalize. My friends, what an intoxicant is democracy. This spring the seeds of democracy have been planted. It may take years, decades, before the peoples of those countries may sit in the shade, but sit in the shade of democracy they someday will.

The biggest of Big Brothers is increasingly helpless because information is the oxygen of the modern age. The peoples of the world have increasing access to this knowledge. It seeps through the walls topped with barbed wire. It wafts across the electrified borders. Breezes of electronic beams blow through the Iron Curtain as if it were lace. And the eventual consequences of this are clear for the people of those countries. To paraphrase the words of John, they shall know the truth and the truth shall set them free.

Truth, which is what Father von Balthasar always sought, is what the totalitarian state has always feared. But totalitarianism didn't anticipate technological change. It didn't foresee televisions, satellite dishes, computers, modems, VCR's, tape recorders, fax machines, copying machines and the beams and pulses of knowledge they give off.

It didn't know that technology would be portable and easily available and thus expand the powers of the individual more than the powers of the state. It didn't know that the modern economy would become dependent on information, relegating to the backwater any country that denies information to its people. It didn't see what the poet W.H. Auden saw: that the true men of action of our time, those who transform the world, are not the politicians, the statesmen, the social planners, but the scientists.

Technology will make it increasingly difficult for the state to limit the information that its people receive. Trying to control the flow of information is a hopeless, desperate cause. Some countries, of course, still try. They fear the flow of information because they fear the truth. In (sic) Rumania, typewriters must be licensed, a laughable proposition as doomed to eventual failure as Rumania's own system of government. In spite of the progress being made through *glasnost*, the Soviet Union in

April revised its criminal code to make it an offense, punishable by up to seven years in prison, for Soviet citizens to accept printers or copying machines from foreigners. Soviet officials still think if they control the paper an idea is carried on they can control the idea.

At one Soviet publisher, you have to get two signatures and submit what you want to copy before you can use the copying machine. At another place, the deputy director of security must give you his written permission, a process that takes two or three days.

These countries and others face an agonizing choice. They can either open their societies to the freedoms necessary for the pursuit of technological advance, or they can risk falling even further behind. They are in a quandary. To enter the information age, which is the direction their economies must head, they must allow for the flow of information. But to allow information undermines central authority and the very political organization of their societies.

Father von Balthasar stood for the concept that moral principles can be discerned by reason. Totalitarianism is an unreasonable and immoral state hostile to every belief our departed member valued. And if Father von Balthasar and I had known each other, I would have told him what I have outlined for you today. Ladies and gentlemen, I am more optimistic than ever in my life about peace and democracy in this world. These are the days of the triumph of freedom and knowledge.

Thank you for this honor and God bless you.

Ronald Reagan

About the Author


Harry E. Winter was born on Dec. 18, 1937, in Norwich, NY.

Perpetual vows in the Missionary Oblates of Mary Immaculate, Roviano, Italy, Sept. 8, 1961.

Priesthood, Rome, Italy, December 16, 1964.

Licentiate in theology, Gregorian University, Rome, Italy, June, 1965.

Instructor, theology, Oblate College (Seminary), Washington, DC, 1965-67.

PhD studies, University of Pennsylvania, Philadelphia, PA, 1967-70; doctorate awarded, December, 1976 (thesis: <u>Catholic, Evangelical and Reformed: the Lord's Supper in the (United) Presbyterian Church, USA, 1945-70</u>).

Professor, philosophy and theology, Oblate College (Cluster of Independent Theological Schools), Washington, DC, 1970-75.

Associate director, Texas Conference of Churches, 1977-79.

Pastor, churches in Virginia, West Virginia and North Carolina, 1979-94; served ecumenical commissions in each diocese.

Professor, Oblate College, 1994-96; President, 1996-97; founder, Oblate Center for Mission Studies.

Pastor, St. Rose of Lima Catholic Church, Buffalo, NY, 1998-